RISKY BUSINESS:
A MAINE VILLAGE GOES GLOBAL

Castine souls and ships during the golden age of sail

Unknown artist, Ship *J. P. Whitney*, at the port of Malta, 1864. Courtesy Custom House Maritime Museum, Newburyport, Massachusetts, Gift of Bernice B. Avery

RICHARD M. AMES

Risky Business: A Maine Village Goes Global
Copyright © 2019 Richard M. Ames

ISBN: 978-1-947758-28-5

On the cover: Attributed to Francis Hustwick, ship *Castine*, built at Castine, Maine and launched in 1857 by Samuel T. Noyes. Here shown outward bound from Liverpool with Holyhead Mountain off the port bow and the Skerries Lighthouse visible off the stern. Private Collection.

This publication accompanies the 2019/2020 exhibit, *Risky Business: Square-Rigged Ships and Salted Fish* organized by the Castine Historical Society, Castine, Maine. www.castinehistoricalsociety.org.

Designed and produced by:
Custom Museum Publishing
12 High Street, Thomaston, Maine
www.custommuseumpublishing.com

Printed in the United States of America

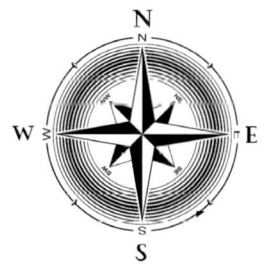

Contents

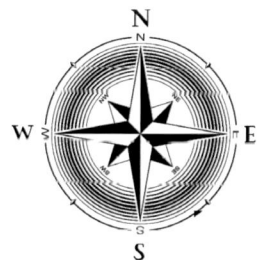

An Introduction to *Risky Business: A Maine Village Goes Global*

It should come as no surprise that Castine, Maine became a bustling location of maritime trade in the 1800s. Castine proved to be a near perfect location for a myriad of ocean related commerce. The deep water adjacent to the shoreline provided an excellent location for ship building, allowing for ships of even the deepest drafts to be slipped down the ways into the harbor. The protected harbor and adjacent Smith Cove provided safe refuge for vessels large and small, and continues to do so even to this day. Proximity to Maine's forests supplied the shipyards with quality boat lumber and mast stock as well as lumber for export. An impressive eighteen full-rigged ships, the ocean going merchant ships of the day, were launched from Castine shipyards. In addition to a thriving ship building port, Castine, situated in the heart of Penobscot Bay's productive fishing grounds, was second only to Portland in supplying the region's large offshore fleet of fishing vessels.

A thriving seaport needs mariners; sea captains, ship's officers, common sailors, carpenters, and cooks. As a professor of Marine Transportation at Castine's Maine Maritime Academy, training the next generation of ship's officers, I am compelled to compare today's aspiring mariners with their counterparts of the 1800s. The book's title phrase, *"Risky Business"*, captures the essence of a seafaring career in the age of ocean trade under sail. Severe weather, piracy, illness, financial temptations, and the realities of the hard life at sea took a toll on 1800s sailors. Ships returning from a yearlong trade route often did so having lost sailors during their passage, or worse, not having returned at all. When a ship carried too much sail, the call to "Take in the royal, take in the t'gallant," sent sailors to climb the ratlines to the upper hamper, lay out on the yards, and haul in sail. Safety gear—unheard of, simply don't let go. Overboard, whether from a fall from aloft or swept from the deck awash, there was no turning back. The square riggers were downwind vessels, maneuvers to retrieve a lost sailor would not have been attempted. Piracy lay claim to many vessels along the well-traveled merchant routes, but privateers may have had a greater impact on the merchant fleet. Foreign governments commissioned private vessels to attack and take the merchant ships of enemy states. It was not uncommon for privateers to expand their reach beyond an enemy state and seize any ship encountered. Even in calm and friendly seas, the risk of illness was ever present. Poor hygiene and sanitation, vermin, and viruses could quickly infect an entire crew in their confined living space. Small pox, yellow fever, typhus, and typhoid headline a list of devastating and sometimes fatal illnesses.

America is a maritime nation. From the country's inception, commercial vessels have provided, and continue to provide, the essential transportation links, work platforms, and coastal connections that sustain our economy. The New Bedford whalers, Castine's square-rigged ships, and the coastwise schooners of the past have evolved to today's massive container ships, supertankers, and a growing coastal workboat fleet. Our future mariners, the young men and women at Maine Maritime Academy, will confront the many inherent perils of the sea as did previous Castine sailors. The power of the sea must still be respected and the possibility of a maritime casualty remain. However, much of the risk of a career at sea today has been mitigated through international and domestic regulation, rigorous training and certification, navigation and communication technology, accessible and reliable weather forecasting, and a robust rescue service network. Today's mariners are competent and confident in their trade.

Like experienced masters and sailors from Penobscot Bay in the 1800s, today's midshipmen set off to sea for their livelihood and adventure. Adventure implies a journey into the unknown where there is the element of risk. The merchant fleet has evolved from wood to steel, sail to power, and sextant to satellite, but the common bond of a career at sea is shared by sailors past and present. *"Risky Business: A Maine Village Goes Global"* offers an intriguing glimpse into the age of commerce under sail and the men and women who took to sea. Enjoy!

Capt. Richard Miller
Associate Professor of Marine Transportation
Maine Maritime Academy
Castine, Maine

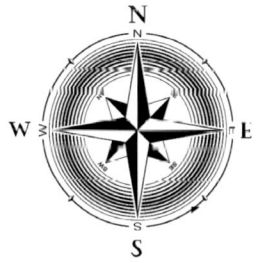

Preface

Most families have that odd bird who is interested in family history and the past. I happen to be one of those people and for many years have engaged in researching and writing about family history.

Pondering what sparked this interest I recall fond memories of Castine summers staying with my grandparents at the Whitney house which was built in 1810 for Captain Henry Whitney and his wife Lucy. This stately home on Castine's Town Common had passed down through the generations, daughter to daughter, and was owned by my grandmother Harriet Hatch Ames. The house was well loved and remained filled with the possessions and memories of multiple generations. Great-uncle Frank (Francis Whiting Hatch), who could spin a yarn with the best of them, would stop by for his daily visits and after back-garden searches for stray golf balls we would wander through the house. Paintings, furniture and knickknacks became the stimulus for fascinating tales of family history. Portraits of ships especially captured my attention. There was something alluring about these majestic vessels with the sun reflecting off their square-rigged sails, colorful flags flapping in the breeze and tiny figures standing on deck preparing for arrival at a distant port.

This fascination with full-rigged ships, and our family's connection with them, led to the research that resulted in this book. I was very fortunate to have original documents carefully preserved by previous generations to reveal first person accounts. In addition, the expanding availability of historical content on the internet provided abundant material.

Risky Business: A Maine Village Goes Global relates stories of people and ships from Castine that contributed to a young America coming onto the global stage. We learn that romanticized portraits of ships calmly sailing in untroubled waters were a depiction of the exception rather than the rule. Operating these ships was arduous and risky work. These majestic vessels and their crews were buffeted not only by weather but also by powerful political and economic forces. However, the resolute men and women of Castine were equal to these challenges and prospered despite the hardships that confronted them. We are also reminded that countless individuals who contributed to this success have gone undocumented.

This book would not have been possible without the assistance of many. Firstly, I would like to thank my wife, Laura Ames, for her patience and understanding as I spent countless hours engrossed in another world researching and writing. I would also like to recognize George Hatch, who kindly agreed to slog through an early draft of the book and who provided insightful suggestions on how to make the subject more relatable. And finally, I would like to acknowledge Lynn Parsons, Paige Lilly and Lisa Simpson Lutts who helped with the formidable task of editing and the Castine Historical Society for making publication possible.

In conclusion, I sincerely hope that reading this book is a pleasurable experience and that you come away with a better understanding of the souls and ships that contributed to Castine's prosperity during the golden age of sail.

Richard M. Ames
Kiawah Island, 2019

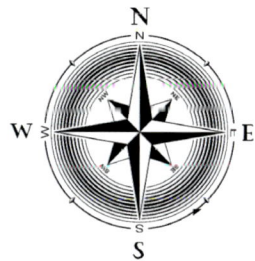

Castine Today and in 1860

Looking out over Castine's waterfront today the coastline is dominated by the Maine Maritime Academy's ship *State Of Maine*, the Town Dock and Eaton's Boatyard. In the harbor itself numerous pleasure vessels bob peacefully at their moorings. Castine's population in the most recent census was 1366, including the 850 Maine Maritime Academy students. During the summer months, when the vacationers arrive, the population swells to about 2500. Most of the travel to and from the Castine peninsula is by road, with the waterfront primarily geared towards recreation.

The Castine of 1860 had a similar sized population of 1357 but was a much busier place. As the business center for the Penobscot Customs District, Castine was the main port for supplying the fishing fleets from the middle third of Maine's coast. Castine's bustling waterfront at this time was dominated by shipyards, wharves, numerous shops, warehouses and salt sheds.[1]

During Castine's glory years of 1840 to 1865, the town and waterfront experienced an annual cycle of profitable activity. Starting in April, up to 500 fishing schooners would arrive in the harbor and wait their turn to take on salt and supplies sold to them by Castine merchants.[2] During the summer months, larger ships loaded with cargoes of salt would arrive from the European ports of Liverpool, England and Cadiz, Spain, to replenish the depleted salt sheds. In the late summer, the fishing schooners would return to unload barrels and boxes of salted cod, mackerel and herring into the waterfront warehouses.

Castine 2018, Map Data: Google

---

1. *Maine Register, State Year-book and Legislative Manual*, No. 38, June 1907, 493.
2. George Brown Goode, *The Fisheries and Fishery Industries of the United States*, (Washington: Government Printing Office, 1887), 36.

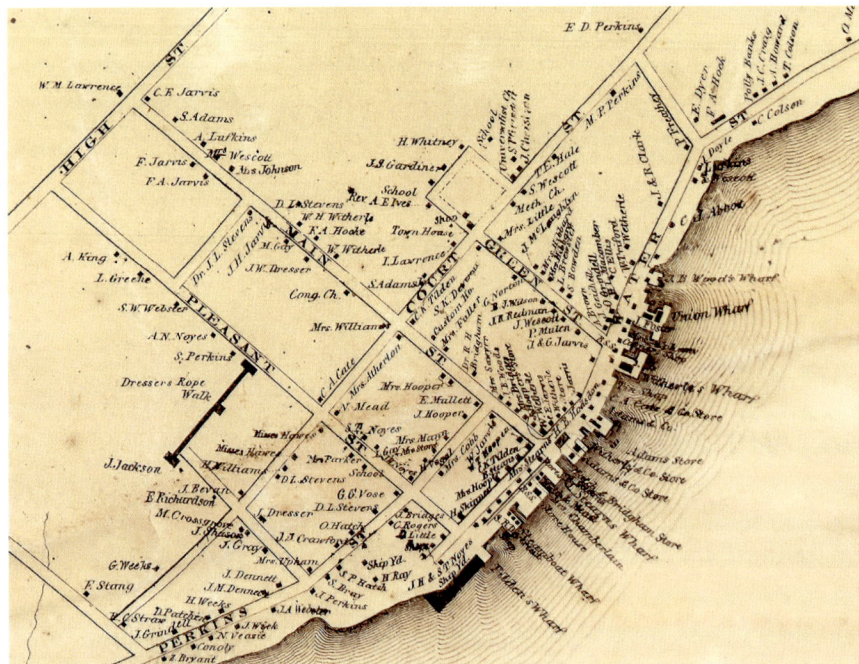

Inset, Topographical Map of Hancock County, Maine, surveys by H. F. Walling (New York: Lee and Marsh, 1860). Private Collection.

In the autumn, Castine built and owned full-rigged ships would arrive to be loaded with salted fish, timber and local farm produce to be transported for sale at southern ports. On January 1st Castine and the harbor would again be a major hub of activity when the fishermen arrived to collect their bounty paid by the U.S. Government to encourage cod fishing.[3] January through March would be relatively quiet months and then the cycle would start anew.

Samuel V. Homan, *View of Castine, Maine, from Hospital Island* (Boston: Bouve and Sharp, Lithographers, 1843). Private Collection.

---

3. In 1819 the cod bounty rate was increased for Maine fishermen and was divided amongst the vessel owners and the crew with 3/8 going to the owners and 5/8 to the crew. The cod bounty was repealed in 1866.

To support this activity, the harbor front was significantly more built up than it is today. In 1860 at the foot of Pleasant Street, where the *State of Maine* is currently docked, was the J. H. & S. T. Noyes Ship Yard which built many of the full-rigged trading ships launched from Castine. Moving towards Main St. were Tilden's Wharf, Steamboat Wharf, J. Stearn's Wharf as well as several stores and warehouses. The brick building at Water and Main Streets, where Camden National Bank is today, housed the merchant and fishing outfitting stores of Adams & Co. and Witherle & Co. On the waterfront between Main and Green streets were the busy wharves of Adams & Co. and Witherle's Wharf. Between Green and Dyer streets were the Union and J. B. Wood's wharves and more shops and warehouses.

Although the commerce of Castine during this period was focused on outfitting local fishing fleets, the town also proudly displayed a cosmopolitan flair. The ladies of Castine were known to wear dresses made from fashionable European fabrics and the homes of merchants and ship captains were filled with fine European furniture and household goods. Remembering Castine during this period Reverend George Adams wrote:

In the summer came ships with cargoes of salt from Liverpool and Cadiz, —sometimes the ships owned here, sometimes French ships or barks with their red-capped sailors, giving to the delighted boys of the town our first lesson in a foreign tongue.[4]

The arrival of sailors in the bustling port of Castine must also have contributed to less genteel activity in the town's waterfront taverns and boarding houses, adding to the excitement of these days gone by.

Fitz Henry Lane, detail of *Castine from Hospital Island*, 1855. Courtesy of Cape Ann Museum, Gloucester, Massachusetts.

---

4.   George Moulton Adams, *Castine Sixty Years Ago: A Historical Address*, (Boston: Press of Samuel Usher, 1900).

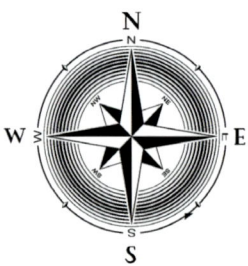

Early Years of Castine

From the early 1600s to the late 1700s Castine was occupied by French, Dutch (briefly), English and then colonial American settlements. The population of the Maine coast did not really see significant growth until the Tariff Act of 1789 was enacted to stimulate the young American economy that had fallen into depression after the Revolutionary War. This act established advantageous tariffs for American shipping and reserved the coastal trade exclusively for American-flagged vessels. The Tariff Act provided the desired stimulus, and adventurous souls moved to the timber rich coast of Maine. The settlers supported themselves by farming the rocky soil and harvesting lumber to build their houses and sailing vessels for fishing.

From 1800 to 1830, growth in American shipping was limited by French and British trade embargoes and war. In 1806 the French forbade allied and neutral ships from trading with Britain. Under these conditions, French men-of-war and privateers considered American-flagged vessels fair game and hunted them down to capture for prize money. Great Britain responded in 1807 with legislation forbidding French trade with Britain and its allies or neutrals and instructed the Royal Navy to blockade French and allied ports.

The Castine Historical Society's logo depicts flags from four nations that once held sway over the town (French, Dutch, British and American).

During this time, Britain was in desperate need of sailors for its war-depleted navy and declared the right to stop and search American vessels for so-called "British deserters." The label of deserter was liberally applied, and large numbers of sailors were forcibly removed from American ships to serve in the British navy. Although American seafarers despised this practice, England was by far America's largest trading partner and the northeast Maritime Provinces were willing to tolerate this injustice to preserve their handsome profits. Representatives from the southern states, however, were not so tolerant and succeeded in imposing a foreign trade embargo into law in 1807. This shut down lucrative international trade and all that remained for law-abiding American vessels was the less profitable coastal trade.

America lifted its foreign trade embargo in 1809 but Britain was still preventing American trade with France. In response to Britain's damaging restrictions on trade and impressments of American seamen into the Royal Navy, the United States declared war on Britain in 1812. The war, which lasted until 1815, included the British occupation of Castine and further deprived opportunities for American vessels.

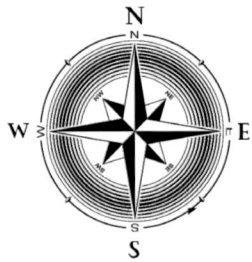

Boom Years of Castine—Fish and Ships

Demand for American shipping started to improve in 1830 when Britain opened West Indies (Caribbean) ports to American trade. This trend accelerated as the manufacturing economies in Europe increased their appetite for American cotton. To satisfy this burgeoning trade, British Navigation Laws were repealed, allowing British merchants to utilize superior and more cost-efficient American-flagged ships for their cargoes.

A growing need for the construction of wooden sailing vessels for fishing and trade had a very positive impact on the fortunes of coastal Maine. Castine, with a deep-water port and proximity to rich fishing grounds, became the center for the Penobscot Bay Region, which dominated tonnage of fishing vessels owned in Maine from 1835 to 1860.[5] Trade during this period primarily consisted of transporting salted fish from Castine to southern ports and then shipping cotton to Europe. This commerce generated considerable profits and Castine became known as the "wealthiest town in Maine in proportion to its size."[6]

Shipbuilding in Maine peaked in 1855 and then started to decline, as cargoes became difficult to secure and freight rates fell. This downward trend continued with the financial panic of 1857, which caused British merchants to withdraw their funds from American banks, severely restricting sources of financing.

In 1861 increasing tensions between the North and South over slavery led to the outbreak of the Civil War. Southern ports were blockaded by the Union navy, and Confederate commerce raiders hunted down and burned vessels hailing from northern ports. The war increased insurance rates for American ships thereby creating a cost advantage for foreign vessels. A large portion of the American merchant fleet was sold abroad.

After the Civil War, increasing dominance of steel and steam reduced the demand for wooden sailing vessels bringing an end to Castine's golden era of sail.

---

5. Wayne M. O'Leary, *Maine Sea Fisheries, The Rise and Fall of a Native Industry, 1830–1890,* (Northeastern University Press, 1996), 350, 351.

6. A. J. Coolidge and J. B. Mansfield, *A History and Description of New England, General and Local,* vol. 1, (Boston: Austin J. Coolidge, 1859), 90.

Fitz Henry Lane, *Castine, Maine*, 1856. Oil on canvas, Museum of Fine Arts, Boston, Massachusetts, Bequest of Maxim Karolik, 64.437, photograph © 2019.

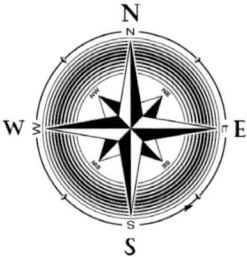

Sailing Vessels Built at Castine

Records for 19th-century ship building are incomplete but identify 122 sailing vessels of various rigs built at Castine. From smallest to largest there were:[7]

4 Sloops	70 Schooners	23 Brigs
(45 to 95 tons)	**(8 to 300 tons)**	**(125 to 357 tons)**

6 Barks	1 Barkentine	18 Ships
(349 to 646 tons)	**(633 tons)**	**(199 to 1178 tons)**

This book focuses on the eighteen full-rigged ships built at Castine between 1803 and 1857.[8] A full-rigged ship is a three masted sailing vessel with square sails on each mast. The most famous and romanticized ships are the "clippers" that came into prominence in the early 1840s to serve a growing demand for rapid delivery of tea from China. The demand for speed continued with the discovery of gold in California and Australia in 1848 and 1851, with prospectors willing to pay a premium to secure passage on fast ships. Clippers were mostly built in Boston and New York while more practical Maine builders constructed sturdier and rounder ships known as Down Easters. Although Down Easters were termed "tubs and slow

---

7.   Images from *Merchant Vessels of the United States*, (United States Coast Guard, Washington, U.S. Govt. print off., 1888).

8.   William Armstrong Fairburn; Ethel M Ritchie, *Merchant Sail*, (Center Lovell, Maine: Fairburn Marine Educational Foundation, 1945–55), 3459.

pokes" by New York and Boston shipowners, "these ships not only made money steadily but also made consistently fair passages, were more reliable than the clippers, were better sea boats, and delivered their cargoes in better physical condition."[9]

Full-Rigged Ships Built at Castine in the 19th Century[10,11,12]				
Name	Year Built	Year Sold or Out of Service	Freight Capacity (tons)	Dimensions (ft.)
Ruthy	1803	1812 seized by a French privateer	199	94 x 25 x 7
Thucydides	1808	1811 lost on the east coast of Ireland, 16 miles south west of Dublin	250	Unknown
Atticus	1819	1833 last reference leaving New York for New Orleans	291	98 x 26 x 13
Canova	1823	1833 sold in Boston	344	111.0 x 25.2 x 13.1
Antioch	1826	1841 sunk at Port Joli, Nova Scotia	395	114.8 x 27.7 x 13.8
Lucas	1828	1833 last reference in Lloyds Register of Shipping	280	102 x 25 x 12
St. Leon	1835	1852 sunk with load of salt on voyage from Cadiz, Spain to Castine	505	134 x 29 x 14
Adams	1840	1863 sold abroad and renamed *Saguenay.* Home port of Liverpool until 1872	592	143.0 x 31.0 x 15.0
William Jarvis	1848	1860 wrecked off Key West, Florida	668	142.3 x 32.1 x 16.1
William Witherle	1851	1864 sold abroad and renamed *Selma.* Home port of Hamburg, Germany until 1873	874	161.5 x 34.3 x 17.2
Ostervald	1853	1858 caught fire and sank 250 miles from the mouth of the Mississippi River	950	165.7 x 34.5 x 17.3
J. P. Whitney	1853	1869 sold at Calcutta and sunk in the Indian Ocean the same year	1020	161.1 x 34.3 x 17.2
Benjamin Thaxter	1854	1856 sunk with load of iron from Cardiff for New York	949	172 x 35 x 17
Samuel Adams	1854	1864 sold abroad and renamed *Alfred.* Home port of Newport, England until 1871	1178	183.7 x 37.2 x 18.6
Hezekiah Williams	1856	1857 wrecked near Port Joli, Nova Scotia	1030	163.1 x 34.2 x 17.1
Edward Hyman	1856	1873 sold abroad. Home port of Nantes, France until 1879	1128	180.5 x 35.5 x 17.8
Castine	1857	1884 sold abroad. Home port of Bremen, Germany until 1889	1032	170.3 x 35.0 x 17.6
Picayune	1857	1866 wrecked on Duck Island, Maine	1081	172.2 x 35.0 x 17.5

9. Ibid. 1733.

10. William Armstrong Fairburn; Ethel M Ritchie, *Merchant Sail,* (Center Lovell, Maine: Fairburn Marine Educational Foundation, 1945–5), 3457–3461.

11. George Savary Wasson; Lincoln Colcord, *Sailing Days on the Penobscot,* (Salem, Mass: Marine Research Society, 1932), 309–320.

12. Applebee Collection, Penobscot Marine Museum, Searsport, Maine.

Investing in and operating large full-rigged wooden ships required significant capital, restricting this activity to the town's wealthiest merchants and investors. For example, the ship *Antioch* built at Castine in 1826 for $27,721 equates to $709,000 in today's dollars while the ship *William Witherle* built in 1851 for $46,787 equates to $1,550,000.

To reduce the financial risks associated with such large investments, ships tended to be owned in shares by merchants, individual investors and often the ship's captain. A good example is the ship *William Witherle*, which had the following owners: William Witherle, 3/8; Isaiah Wescott, Master, 1/8; Joseph Wescott, 1/8; David L. Stevens, 1/8; Charles Atherton, 1/16; Hezekiah Williams, 1/16; Samuel Noyes, 1/24; Joshua H. Noyes, 1/24; and Samuel T. Noyes, 1/24; of Castine.

Records and references were scoured for information pertaining to these eighteen Castine ships. Enough has been gathered to gain considerable insight into their voyages and how long they sailed the seas. The average lifespan for ships with complete records was fourteen and a half years with the shortest life being one year and the longest being thirty-two years. The stories and events relating to these ships provide interesting insights into 19th-century wooden ship seafaring and shed light on the period that brought considerable growth and prosperity to Castine.

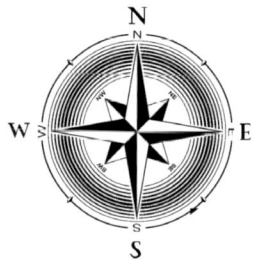

Ship *Thucydides*: Wrecked on the Irish Coast

The ship *Thucydides* was built at Castine in 1808 for James Crawford and others. There is no record of her dimensions, but she most likely had a carrying capacity of about 200 tons similar to the ship *Ruthy* built at Castine five years earlier.

An account of voyages on the *Thucydides* is found in the writings of Lemuel Norton who was born in Edgartown, Martha's Vineyard in 1785. In 1786 his carpenter father moved with the family to Brooksville, Maine to seek new opportunities. At the age of fourteen Lemuel took a job as a printer's apprentice in Castine for the *Castine Journal and Eastern Advertiser*. Although he enjoyed and became proficient at typesetting his attention often wandered to the happenings in the harbor:

Ships, brigs, and schooners, coming in from different parts of the world and anchoring in the harbor, within hailing distance of our office, from time to time, greatly attracted my attention, and their splendid appearance with the men and boys on the yards and at the mast-head, furling and sometimes loosening their sails, drew my affections quite away from my other pursuits, and I longed to be a sailor. My roving propensities overcame me, and I finally came to the conclusion that I would leave the indoor work of setting type, and go and see what was to be seen in other climes and in other kingdoms.

At the age of sixteen Lemuel shipped out on his first voyage:

I packed what little I had of clothing, together with a Bible and Watts' Hymns, and leaving my father's house, went on board the good schooner Polly, of Castine, belonging to Capt. Joseph Perkins of said place, where a berth had been provided for me to go as cook to the West Indies.

After a number of voyages to far off places, including a passage to Havana and back on the Castine-built ship *Ruthy*, Lemuel shipped for Liverpool in 1809 as second officer on the Castine ship *Thucydides*:

The Embargo Law, which still remained in force to some extent, was at this time so modified that vessels could go to England. Consequently, the new ship Thucydides, *which had been built during the embargo, was immediately fitted for sea, and my brother and myself were engaged by the owner, Mr. Crawford, to go out in her as first and second officers.* [13]

Lemuel's brother, who suffered from bad health, died on the return voyage to Boston and was buried at sea. Returning to Castine with salt, the *Thucydides* next loaded with lumber and departed for England in January of 1811 with Lemuel being promoted to first officer. The winter months, known for

---

13. Lemuel Norton, *Autobiography of Lemuel Norton*, (Concord: Fogg, Hadley & Company, 1864), 17–18.

bad weather, lived up to their reputation:

This proved to be a terrible cold and stormy passage. We experienced some severe gales, though our ship made no complaint, but proved herself fully equal to the conflict, being well manned and well managed.

Nothing alarming took place till after we made the land, when sailing up St. George's Channel we made a very small mistake; and in consequence of steering a little too much to the north of east, we had to pass in shore, or to the northward, of the Tuscar Rock, which is a very small island, in shore of which no large vessel ever attempts to pass unless driven to through sheer necessity.[14]

Portrait of Lemuel Norton. From *Auto-Biography of Lemuel Norton: Labors in the Gospel Ministry*, 1864.

The wind being southeasterly and blowing a gale, we could never get so far to windward as we needed to be, on our direct course from Cape Clear to Holyhead. The wind increasing and heading us off, we soon found ourselves nearing the Irish coast, but made out to fetch along shore up the Channel that night till the next morning, when we discovered the land not more than four or five miles under our lee bow. The wind having become fixed, and blowing a gale we ought to have gone into Waterford. But no; our captain was a little too stout for that, and on we sped… the sea breaking over us in a manner almost alarming.

We had already passed by a good harbor, and there was none ahead that we could possibly reach … we must either lighten the ship or shorten sail. If we shortened sail, the ship would inevitably go on shore where we must all perish in the breakers. Accordingly we concluded to lighten the ship of all the lumber, spars, etc., that were on the upper deck.[15]

This being done, our ship seemed to make rather better weather for a time. But alas! the gale increased to a fury, so that we must now reef or carry our masts over the side. With much difficulty a reef was taken in each topsail, and all the staysails furled but the storm staysails. This seemed to relieve the ship a little, though she would plunge fearfully into the sea at times, which was now running mountains high and breaking on the shore to the leeward of us with awful grandeur.[16]

After frantically taking several more actions to keep the *Thucydides* off the rocks the fate of the ship and her crew became clear:

The captain and myself now went on to the fore yard to see if we could discover some place where the ship could be run on shore with some prospect of saving our lives. We were fortunate enough to see a place where we thought she might be run so near the shore without striking, as to render it possible for us to escape. When directly abreast of this chosen spot of life or death, the helm was put hard up, the ship fell off before the sea, and in another moment, as it were, she was flying upon the top of a mighty wave, which carried her so far on shore that when that wave left her, it was as if she had been let fall from some twenty feet in the air, striking with such a fearful crash, and so sudden, that it brought every man flat to the deck. In this fearful moment every man had to look out for himself.

---

14. St. George's Channel is located between Ireland and Wales in the Irish Sea.
15. A spar is a wooden pole used to support sails and rigging. Spare spars were carried by sailing vessels.
16. Lemuel Norton, *Autobiography of Lemuel Norton*, (Concord: Fogg, Hadley & Company, 1864), 85–86.

With the stricken *Thucydides* taking a bashing against the shore, first officer Lemuel devised a plan:

A thought struck my mind just at this juncture of affairs, to make fast a rope to a plank that I had saved when clearing the deck in the morning, and let the sea take it on shore. This was accordingly done, and just at that moment two Irishmen came to the spot, saw, and secured the plank, holding on to the end of the rope.

The rope was successfully used to get all fifteen crew members safely to shore, which turned out to be Cooldross Beach, sixteen miles south-west of Dublin. After making it to dry land, the cold and weary crew were lent assistance by the locals:

…after getting safe on shore and drying ourselves by the fire of a poor Irishman, who lived nearby in a mud hut, and getting some refreshments in a better house nearby, we returned to the ship … and got the small anchor on shore with the cable attached, to prevent the ship from going off in case she should float the next tide.

Valuables recovered from the wreck were piled into a hut and the crew found lodgings for the night in a nearby barn. In the morning, Lemuel discovered that his trunk, with all of his possessions, had been stolen and was disappointed but he was happy to be alive.

The crew remained in the area for a month recovering cargo and stripping the ship of anything of value but the story of the missing trunk was not over:

After being here some days, I told a gentleman who came down to the ship, about losing my trunk, and he said he would try to do something about it for me. Accordingly, he got all the priests in the vicinity, a distance of eight miles from the ship each way, to cry it in their churches. These Catholic priests told their congregations that if any of them had the American mate's trunk, or anything else belonging to the ship, to return it immediately, on pain of being excluded from the church.[17]

The priest's threat did have an impact, but not the desired one, and the man who had earlier offered assistance found the following note on his doorstep:

Dear Sir: In the third crotch of such a tree in your garden you will find the American mate's pocket book.

The empty pocket book, stripped of all money, was returned by the partially repenting thief.

The *Thucydides* was eventually examined by a jury of carpenters from Dublin who determined that she was not worth trying to repair. The wreck was sold where she lay to the highest bidder for a sum of $900.

---

17. Norton, *Autobiography*, 88–93.

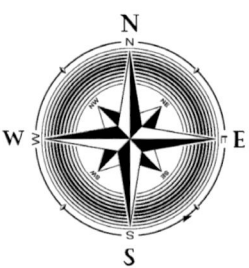

Ship *Atticus*: Pursued by Pirates

Builder's Half Model of the ship *Atticus*, Courtesy of the Smithsonian/NMAH Maritime. The *Atticus* was built at Castine in 1819 and was 291 tons with dimensions of 98'x26'x13'. She was owned by James Crawford and Joseph Wescott of Castine.

The ship *Atticus* represents "a class of such vessels that were developed in New England after the War of 1812 for the foreign trade. Though considered a large merchant vessel at the time of her launching, ships of the size of the *Atticus* were soon very common in the American trade with European and Mediterranean ports."[18]

Profitable trade between the coast of Maine and the islands of the West Indies (Caribbean) was initiated in the 1760s. This trade consisted of Maine vessels departing with local products of lumber, fish and farm produce, and returning with cargoes of molasses, sugar and English manufactured goods.

Pirates infested the Caribbean and Gulf of Mexico, disrupting this trade until the 1830s, when piracy was largely eliminated through intervention by Western European and American navies. During the 1820s there were several accounts of Maine vessels being viciously attacked by pirates. An example of this brutality can be found in an 1823 account from a voyage of the brig *Belisarius* from Kennebunk. When off Campeche after being overrun by pirates, Captain Perkins told them they could take all the money they could find on board. Finding less than they had hoped for, they cut off the captain's right arm, then his left arm, and finally his leg above the knee. To finish him off they filled his mouth with oakum, soaked

---

18. Howard Irving Chapelle, *The National Watercraft Collection*, (Washington: Smithsonian Institution, 1960), 55.

it with oil, and set it on fire.[19]

Another horrific account is from a Miss Lucretia Parker, the only survivor from the English sloop, *Eliza Ann*, which was attacked by pirates in 1825 on a voyage from St. Johns to Antigua. After having been overrun the "motley crew of desperadoes, armed with weapons of almost every description … they commenced their barbarous work by unmercifully beating and maiming all on board except myself." The wounded crew were taken to shore where the pirates again fell on them with swords, knives and axes. The captain, after pleading for mercy, was clubbed with an ax and then stabbed in the heart. The remaining nine crew members were bludgeoned to death by "ferocious monsters whose thirst for blood appeared to be insatiable." Miss Parker was imprisoned in an onshore hut but luckily survived to tell her story as the pirates were captured after attacking a disguised British sloop of war.[20]

The *Atticus* was involved in the West Indies trade and no doubt the captain and crew were well acquainted with tales of the bloodthirsty pirates that hunted in these waters. The following account of Captain Dunbar while master of the *Atticus* is remembered and told by his nephew David Wasson:

Detail of *Piratical barbarity/lines composed by Miss Lucretia Parker, who was a passenger on board the English sloop Eliza-Ann, which was captured by the pirates, March 12, 1825, and the whole crew (ten in number) barbarously murdered in presence of that unfortunate young lady*, broadside, 1825. Courtesy Clements Library, University of Michigan, Ann Arbor, Michigan.

Twenty years ago I was master of the ship Atticus, sailing out of Castine. She would be thought a small ship nowadays, being but of three hundred and ten tons burden, but she was large for those days, and was the fastest ship that ever sailed out of Penobscot Bay. Well that she was so, or I should not be here today.

I was in the West India trade, and having taken in almost one-third of a cargo at windward island, that is, one farthest to the east, was running down to a leeward Island, about six hundred miles, to fill up my ship. One-third of a cargo made a perfect set of ballast for a very heavy wind, so that my ship could but have been in condition to sail faster. And this, too, was providential, as you will soon see; for had she been either fully laden or in light ballast we should have been overhauled and lost.

At that time there were a great many pirates in the West Indian seas. They were merciless creatures, and killed all whom they captured.

If they spared one, he might see them afterwards in Boston or New York, when they came there to spend their money, and so might bear witness against them, and cause them to be punished. In earlier years the pirates were more merciful, but when some had been convicted by chancing to meet persons whom they had spared, the others

19. William Hutchinson Rowe, *The Maritime History of Maine, Three Centuries of Shipbuilding and Seafaring*, (New York: W. W. Norton & Company, 1948), 111.

20. Joseph Lewis French, ed. *Great Pirate Stories*, (New York: Tudor, 1922), 273–290.

said, "Dead men tell no tale," and murdered all whom they took. People who begin to do wickedly almost always have to do another wicked thing to cover the first, and so can never find a stopping place.

One morning when we were about half way to our port, a fair wind was blowing very freshly indeed, and we were running under short sail. At sunrise I came on deck, and took my glass, as I always did the first thing in the morning, to look around and see if any sail were in sight. And far away to the south, straight astern, I could barely discern a schooner standing to the north. I had just barely made her out when her course was changed, and she began sailing directly after us. In a few minutes I saw more sail spread upon her. First a reef was taken out of the topsail, then the topgallant-sail was let down from the fore arm. Evidently she was chasing us.

I did not like to alarm the crew—so I said nothing about the vessel astern, but called the mate and said: "Mr. Masida, it's best to make the most of a fair wind; you may take out the reefs from the topsails, and set the topgallant-sails."

"All hands aloft to make sail!" he shouted. Then coming up to me, looking a little pale, he said: "What is it, captain?" for he had noticed that I had kept the glass at my eye a good while. "Nothing of great consequence," I guess, said I. Something I'm certain, he said to himself, but went away.

I didn't keep the secret long, for when the sailors had done making sail, one of them spied the schooner, and cried, "Sail ho!" They all saw her, and knew in a moment what in meant. Coming down to the deck, they stood in a group, looking pretty anxious, but keeping quiet, and gazing at me as if I carried all their lives in my hands. Before long we could see the schooner plainly from the deck with the naked eye. How swiftly she came on! And we, too, were rushing forward at great speed.

Soon the mate came aft again. "Captain Dunbar, we are ready to set more sail, if you say so." "Not now," said I; we'll see. The wind freshens fast, and I'm not sure we could carry more sail with safety.

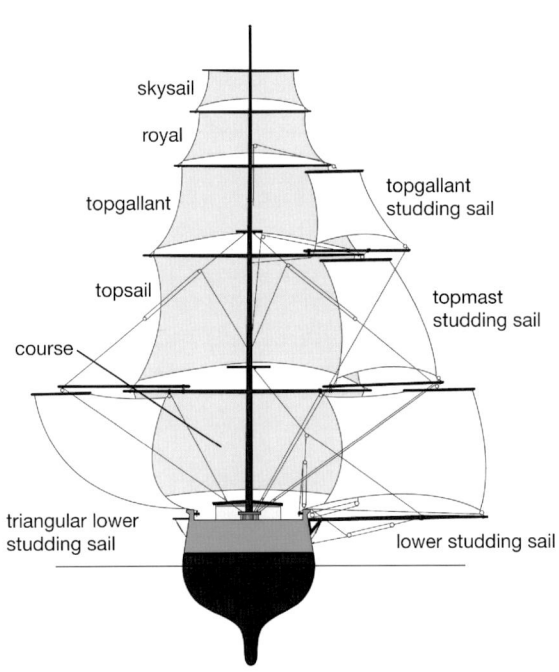

skysail

royal

topgallant

topgallant
studding sail

topsail

topmast
studding sail

course

triangular lower
studding sail

lower studding sail

© 2012 Encyclopædia Britannica, Inc.

Naming of ships sails. Courtesy of Encyclopaedia Britannica, Inc., copyright 2011, used with permission.

In an hour more the pirate was only three or four miles astern. We could see her decks crawled with men. And presently up went the black flag! Yes, there it was, and now if we could out sail the pirate, we lived; if not, we died.

The wind had been freshening fast all the while, and was near a sharp gale. I had never in my life, perhaps, had so much canvas on in a heavy blow, but we must spread more.

"Set the topgallants." You should have seen the men fly to obey. They had the canvas up in about the time it commonly takes a seaman to shift his quid of tobacco from one cheek to the other.

"Set the royals." It was done almost as soon as said. I now waited to see if we were going fast enough; but soon perceived, only too plainly, that the pirate still gained upon us, though slowly at last. I looked up to the masts. They were bending like coach-whips—that they did not go overboard seemed a miracle—and yet we must carry more sail.

"Get on the studding sails," I said; we must trust God to make the ship bear it. At any other time had I ordered the seamen aloft when the masts were threatening each moment to go by the board, they would have refused duty; now they sprang up the shrouds like cats. Studding-sail after studding-sail was set; then we got out the boats' sails, and spread them wherever they would catch a capful of wind. And still not a spar nor yard parted. It seemed to me that they were held only by the mighty power of God.

There were a few moments of deep suspense. I stood turning by eye now aloft at the bending, groaning masts, then astern at our fierce pursuer.

"Courage, boys", I cried; she no longer gains. What a hurrah! But the next moment they were still as death again, for it did not seem possible that the top-hamper could hold out; and the snapping of one spar or rope would have doomed us.

And so for an hour that seemed like a year. The ship flew, but the moments lagged—how they lagged! Still the wind increased. I could see that the pirate was ploughing terribly into the sea, and that if the wind went on increasing she must soon take in sail. Presently there was a puff of smoke at her bow, and a cannon-ball plunged into the sea a quarter of a mile astern. The men quailed a little, but I said, "Good Boys!" they begin to see that they cannot catch us.

Soon another ball, which went farther, but was wild. She kept firing for half an hour. Some of the balls would have struck, had they been well enough aimed, but the firing hindered her speed, and she lost ground considerably.

It was now nine o'clock. By this time the gale was too much for her, and her great square sail was taken in. She fell astern rapidly; at one o'clock her hull could no longer be seen, and she gave up the chase, hauling to and shortening sail. I now had the studding-sails and royals taken in, and ordered dinner, for as yet no man had tasted food. We soon left her out of sight. But if God didn't hold our masts in that day, I don't know what did.[21]

Fortunately, the *Atticus* performed well, and she was able to out-sail the pursuing blood-thirsty pirates, allowing Captain Dunbar and his crew to return to Castine to tell this tale. In addition to serving the West Indies trade, the *Atticus* sailed to European ports, as there are records of a 56-day voyage from Le Havre, France to Charleston, South Carolina in 1826; a voyage from St. Ubes, Portugal (a salt loading port) to Penobscot, Maine in 1827 and a voyage from Le Havre, to New Orleans, Louisiana in 1832.

---

21. David A. Wasson, *Golden Argosy*, vol. 3, (New York, August 29, 1885), 312.

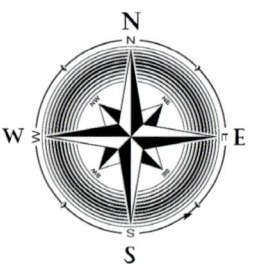

Ship *Canova*: The Castine Triangle

F. A. Perkins, ship *Canova*, 1823. Courtesy Penobscot Marine Museum, Searsport, Maine, acc. 213. The *Canova* was built at Winterport in 1823 and towed to Castine by row boats, where she was rigged and finished for a total cost of $18,009. She had a freight capacity of 344 tons and dimensions of 111' x 26' x 13'. Owners were Witherle & Jarvis ½ and Thomas Adams ½ of Castine. She was armed with two cannons, one of which is mounted today at the foot of Main Street in Castine.

Castine's Henry Whitney, who completed his stately home at the head of the Castine Common in 1810, was master of the ship *Canova* from its maiden voyage in 1823 until 1831. Joseph Wescott, also of Castine, was in command of the *Canova* from 1831 until 1833, when she was sold in Boston.

"Triangle trade" is the name given to repeated voyages between three destinations and one of the most famous trade triangles of the 19th century was known as the "cotton triangle." The cotton triangle involved ships sailing from New York with ballast or general freight to the southern ports of New Orleans, Charleston, Savannah, or Mobile. Next, they loaded cotton and sailed across the Atlantic to a European port. Once there, they returned to New York with immigrants or general merchandise.

Starting in the 1820s Castine-based merchants developed their own version of the triangle trade to satisfy demand for massive quantities of salt required to cure fish caught by the Penobscot Region fishing fleet. In the first leg of the Castine triangle, locally owned ships exported fish, timber and farm produce to the southern ports of New Orleans, Charleston or Savannah. The second leg involved loading cotton at these ports and transporting it to Europe, most commonly Liverpool, England and Le Havre, France. In the final leg of the triangle salt was loaded at Liverpool or Cadiz, Spain, and brought back to Castine.

Ship *Canova* cannon, Main Street, Castine, Maine. Photograph by Richard Ames.

Unknown artist, Portrait of Captain Henry Whitney (1783-1837), c. 1807. Private Collection.

The imported salt was stored in large salt houses built on the Castine wharves and was sold by the ton to the fishing fleet. In the heyday of fishing it was not uncommon to see hundreds of schooners waiting in Castine harbor to load salt and other provisions.

Records from the *Canova*, with Captain Henry Whitney at the helm, are the earliest documentation of a Castine ship sailing the fish-cotton-salt triangle. On her maiden voyage in May of 1823 the *Canova* departed Castine arriving in Charleston after fifteen days at sea. The voyage across the Atlantic, to the port of Liverpool, was completed in forty days. She then returned to Castine with 431 tons of salt. This trip set a pattern that was followed by other Castine ships for decades.[22]

An example of the goods transported from Castine to southern cotton ports is found in an invoice for the cargo shipped on the *Canova* in November 1823:

32,000 ft. Joists; 42,000 ft. White Pine Boards; 100 Spruce Spars; 127 Barrels Potatoes; 355 Boxes Codfish; 100 Boxes Alewives; 651 Boxes Smoked Herring; 17 Barrels Mackerel; 21 Barrels Cod Oil; 4 Barrels Pickled Codfish.[23]

Castine owners of the *Canova*, Thomas Adams and Witherle & Jarvis, always had an interest in landing salt at Castine but also had a keen eye on maximizing their profits. This is evidenced by the following let-

---

22. Wayne M. O'Leary, "The Maine Transatlantic Salt Trade in the Nineteenth Century," *The American Neptune*, vol. 47, No. 2, (1987), 90.

23. Invoice of cargo shipped on *Canova*, November 1823 voyage from Castine to Charleston. Castine Historical Society collection of transcribed *Canova* documents.

ter to Captain Whitney, in November of 1825, instructing him to make two Atlantic crossings before returning to Castine with salt—unless there were more advantageous opportunities:

Dear Sir,

You will proceed with the Ship Canova to New Orleans dispose of your Cargo on owners account and remit the proceeds (excepting sufficient for necessary expenses) to Messrs Rice & Thaxter of Boston. Our object is to employ the Canova in the freighting business and you have liberty to proceed to any part of the world— which you may think for our interest. You will endeavour to make such arrangements as will enable you to take two freights to Europe if possible during the season and return to this place

Henry and Lucy Perkins Whitney House, built in 1810. Courtesy Castine Historical Society.

the next fall with a Cargo of Liverpool salt. We observe here that a cargo of salt will pay us about $2500 freight —and the direction to return to this place with salt is not to be regarded if the Ship can do better.

If freight abroad cannot be had you will of course be obliged to do the best you can Coastwise—remembering that in our opinion freights to Europe are more profitable than coastwise freights, on account of the increased Port Charges. Make remittance as directed above, as you are able, always reserving sufficient for current expenses and let it be done in a safe paper, and to best advantage having regard to the rate of Exchange. Address yourself to Houses of known respectability and on no account form any connection with those of opposite character. Keep us constantly informed of your proceedings.

In this same letter, we learn the details of Captain Whitney's compensation:

You are to receive Fifty Dollars per month, Primage on freight obtained. One half the net proceeds of Cabin freight or Passengers, and 2 ½ % on the net sale of your cargo at New Orleans.[24]

Ship *Canova* Stern Board. Private Collection.

Primage refers to a percentage of the freight value, typically 5%, paid to the master for his care and trouble. Carrying freight or passengers in the captain's cabin was also rewarded. Calculations for an 1824 *Canova* voyage from New Orleans to Le Havre, with 1101 bales of cotton, show that the primage and cabin freight components were worth significantly more to Captain Whitney than his monthly

---

24.   Letter from Witherle & Jarvis to Captain Henry Whitney, November 30, 1825. From Castine Historical Society collection of transcribed *Canova* documents.

salary. The two-month voyage, including loading and unloading time, resulted in a total compensation for Captain Whitney of $948, broken down in the following table:

Ship's Captain Compensation 1824	
Compensation Component	Compensation
Primage (5% on freight obtained)	$360.00
Cabin Freight (1/2 of net proceeds on 28 cotton bales stuffed in the Captain's cabin)	$488.00
Salary (two months)	$100.00
Total Compensation	$948.00
Total Compensation in today's money	$25,000.00

This calculation demonstrates that successful ship's captains were handsomely compensated for their multifaceted skills allowing many of them to construct stately Castine homes that still proudly bear their names.

After a profitable service of ten years the ship *Canova*, a pioneer of the Castine trade triangle, was sold to Benjamin T. Reed & Christopher Hall of Boston in October 1833 for $8,500.

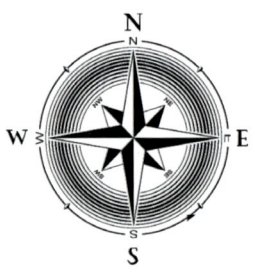

Ship *Antioch*: Trouble 'Tween-Decks'

Elford's Signal Flag Code for the ship *Antioch*. Courtesy Castine Historical Society.

The ship *Antioch* was built at Castine in 1826 by Samuel Noyes for a cost of $27,721. She had a freight capacity of 395 tons and dimensions of 115' x 28' x 14'. Owners were John H. Jarvis, William Witherle, and Thomas Adams of Castine and Sylvanus Rich Jr. of Bucksport. Her home port was Castine.

A trunk in the attic of Captain Whitney's Castine home yielded a book entitled *Marine Telegraph*, by James Elford. Inside the front cover is an inscription and illustration from the author:

Ship Antioch of Castine Designating Signal 53–21. Please hoist your signal as above when coming into or going out of any Port, also on Sundays while in Port.

Signal flags were developed to identify ships from a distance and to communicate short messages. Elford's signals were:

...composed as to enable vessels at sea, provided with only two sets of the six telegraphic flags, to make 7569 signals for the merchant service.[25]

Elford's flag codes were easy to read and were used in Boston Harbor and along the Atlantic Seaboard from 1823 to 1857.

During the 1830s the number of people seeking to emigrate to America, the land of new opportunities, dramatically increased. Previously, ships arriving to European ports with cotton would typically make the return voyage to the United States loaded with salt and manufactured goods. The increased demand for carrying passengers, however, provided a profitable alternative, and many ships returned with human cargo. American ships were preferred by agents and passengers alike as

---

25. James Elford, *Marine Telegraph*, Charleston: James M. Elford, (1823).

they had a reputation for being larger, better built and sailed by more skilled and humane captains and crews.[26]

Most emigrants were poor and booked the cheapest rates in steerage or 'tween-decks' which were names given to the space above the cargo hold and below the main deck. In steerage, bunks were constructed on the starboard and port sides and if room permitted, eating tables with benches were built along the central aisle. Ventilation was provided by hatches in the ceiling to the upper deck that had to be closed during rough weather.

Due to the ever-present danger of fire, cooking facilities were located in a small room on the upper deck with the fire itself built on a bed of earth and stones. An iron grate was placed over the fire with hooks above it for hanging pots.

THE EMBARKATION, WATERLOO DOCKS LIVERPOOL

Embarkation of an Emigrant Ship, Liverpool, from *The Illustrated London News,* July 6, 1850.
Courtesy Illustrated London News Ltd/Mary Evans.

The daily schedule for steerage passenges was very regimented. After being woken up at 6 or 7 am the first chore of the day was to clean their living quarters. Next, designated cooks for groups of 8–12 people, were allowed on deck in shifts to prepare breakfast. This process was repeated for lunch at 1 pm and dinner at 6 pm. In fair weather meals were eaten on deck. In bad weather, access to cooking facilities on deck was not permitted and passengers were confined below.

---

26. James M. Bergquist, *Daily Life in Immigrant America,* 1820–1870, (Westport: The Greenwood Press, 2008), 70.

Passengers were also bound by a strict set of rules which required them to keep the peace and prohibited shouting, cursing, inciting arguments and fighting. The first mate or captain was designated to settle any disputes amongst passengers.

The voyage across the Atlantic, depending on the weather and port of destination, lasted thirty-five to fifty days. During the voyage, particularly during bad weather, lack of hygiene and minimal ventilation resulted in foul smelling and disease-ridden steerage decks. To suppress the stench, sailors were sent below with buckets of tar into which they plunged red hot irons creating a welcomed and overpowering petroleum fragranced steam which fumigated these areas.

Like many ships of this period, the *Antioch* sometimes carried human freight from European ports. Although this was a profitable endeavor for the owners, it was a less desirable alternative for the captain and crew, as dealing with human cargo presented all kinds of problems. These troubles are evident in communications from Captain Whitney of the *Antioch* to the ship's owners:

Das Mitteldeck eines Auswandererschiffs.

Emigrants at Dinner. Below deck on the emigrant ship St. Vincent from *The Illustrated London News*, April 13, 1844. Courtesy Illustrated London News Ltd/Mary Evans.

> *Liverpool April the 20, 1830*
> *Since I wrote you last I have chartered the ship for New York for £480 sterling to be dispatched on the 5ᵗʰ of May. I am to take as many passengers as the law allows and to lode the ship to 15 ½ feet if required by the charters… I have to take 138 passengers and have 100 on board now and from what I can see I shall have trouble enough but it is too late to repent.*

Captain Whitney is ready for sea fourteen days later and is irritated by the unruly passengers and all their problems:

> *Liverpool May the 4, 1830*
> *I informed you I had chartered the ship for New York for £480 I have got ready for sea and have on board some freight and 137 passengers on board of all sorts and sizes—you may judge the trouble I shall have… I should*

have sent you the amounts of my disbursements but I have been so troubled with the passengers I could not do it but shall send them from New York. I should be pleased to meet M. Jones on my arrival as it is possible I may have trouble with the passengers.[27]

The *Antioch* arrived in New York after a passage of thirty-eight days. The charter fee of £480 equates to $55,600 in today's dollars, demonstrating the level of revenues available from participation in emigrant trade. Captain Whitney, however, was glad to be rid of the passengers and all their problems and looked forward to his next voyage carrying low maintenance cotton.

The *Antioch* met her fate in 1841 on a voyage from Le Havre, France to New Orleans, sinking at Port Jolie, Nova Scotia after a life of fifteen years.

---

27. Letter from Captain Whitney to the *Antioch's* owners, May 4, 1830. Castine Historical Society.

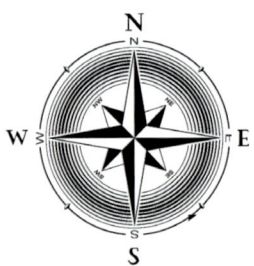

Ship *St. Leon*: Salt from Start to Finish and Oak versus Hackmatack

John Hughes, the ship *St. Leon*, 1838. Courtesy Penobscot Marine Museum, Searsport, Maine, acc. 584. Here shown in 1838 inward bound to Liverpool at the western entrance to the River Mersey with Perch Rock Fort and Lighthouse visible off the starboard bow. Built at Castine in 1835, by Samuel Noyes for a cost of $33,462, she was 505 tons with dimensions of 134' x 29' x 14'. Owners were William Witherle, John H. Jarvis, Thomas Adams and Hezekiah Williams of Castine.

The Penobscot Region during the 19th century was the center of Maine's cod fisheries, and Castine, with its protected deep-water harbor, was the region's main port. Curing the fish caught by the Penobscot Region's substantial fleet required vast quantities of salt. For example, a pound of salt was required to cure every one to two pounds of cod or every two to three pounds of mackerel. In addition, large quantities of salt were required for Castine's shipbuilding industry which, demanded fifty to seventy tons of salt to cure the timbers used in the construction of a large full-rigged ship.[28]

Salt was imported to Castine from European ports and was most commonly loaded directly into the ship's hold. To maximize the value of the cargo, salt was often loaded to a weight exceeding the vessels registered tonnage. This practice rendered salt-carrying a risky proposition for older ships and is mentioned in a letter from a *St. Leon* owner to his partners in 1845. "*My own view is ..... that the ship getting now to be ancient should bring a small cargo—say 700 tons.*" This advice seems to have been followed as the *St. Leon* arrived safely in Castine on voyage with a salt cargo of 660 tons.[29]

Captain Henry Whitney sailed his final voyage as master of the ship *St. Leon*. Arriving at Le Havre in 1837, to load with salt before returning to Castine, he became ill and died there at the age of 57 after an illustrious career at sea. Ironically, ten years later, Henry's daughter, Lucy, joined him at rest in Le Havre. Lucy had married Castine ship captain Moses Gay and like many young wives of ship captains, had chosen a life at sea. She fell ill with smallpox while at Le Havre and died there in 1847, requesting to be laid to rest at her father's side.[30]

Le Havre, c. 1885. Courtesy Antiqua Print Gallery/Alamy Stock Photo.

28. Wayne M. O'Leary, "The Maine Transatlantic Salt Trade in the Nineteenth Century," *The American Neptune*, vol. 47, No. 2, (1987), 83–85.

29. Ibid., 99–100.

30. Henry Austin Whitney, *Incidents in the Life of Samuel Whitney*, (Boston: printed for private distribution, 1860), 84.

Keeping a wooden sailing ship in good working condition required frequent repairs and replacement of worn out or damaged planks and timbers. Insights into the woods used in the construction and repair processes are found in a deposition of Joel Perkins, a ship carpenter and master builder, who worked in Castine shipyards and helped build and repair the *St. Leon*. During the deposition, he was asked:

In your judgment what are the best woods for the construction of vessels, having reference in your answer to both strength and durability?

His answer was:

Hard wood for the bottom, and hackmatack[31] for the top above light water. Hard pine for the ceiling and deck frames, and above the light water mark outside.

When asked to justify his opinion he stated:

In repairing vessels where oak and hackmatack were side by side, I have always found the hackmatack sounder than the oak, in some cases, a very great difference in favor of the hackmatack. I have never known oak to be more sound than hackmatack, in such cases. This is the experience of all the ship builders with whom I am acquainted. The ship "St. Leon" was built about 1834, of the best Merrimac oak and hackmatack. I worked upon her, and know her construction and materials. In 1848 I think it was, I helped repair this vessel. Her bow cants[32] were oak and hackmatack, alternating. The oak we found very rotten, while the hackmatack was per-

fectly sound. The woods being side by side, and bolted together, were subjected to the same exposure. She was ceiled with oak forward, which we found rotten. All the oak which was removed, was replaced with hackmatack. We also found amidships, where oak and hackmatack were used, in proportion two of oak, and one of hackmatack, the oak affected with dry rot, although not badly enough to be removed; while the hackmatack was perfectly bright and sound. The "St. Leon" was built in the summer time, by day's works, for her owners to wear out, and was owned by them until her loss, some fifteen or twenty years ago.[33]

The sturdily-built ship *St. Leon* continued sailing the seas until 1852

John H. Jarvis house on Water Street, Castine. Jarvis was a ship owner and partner in Witherle & Jarvis, 1810–1844. The house was built in the early 1800s; later became the Castine House Inn; the El Dorado Hotel; and burned in 1884. Copy photo courtesy Castine Historical Society.

---

31. Hackmatack also known as tamarack is a bog tree, fast-growing with shallow roots, prized because of its strength and durability in wooden shipbuilding.

32. A bow cant is a curved frame timber at the front of a vessel.

33. *United States Court of Commissioners of Alabama Claims, Records,* 1882–85, vol. 16, 55.

when at an age of seventeen she met her demise carrying 780 tons of salt exceeding her registered tonnage by more than fifty percent.[34] The following account of her sinking was published in *The Sailors Magazine*:

> *Ship St. Leon, Lufkin, of Castine, from Cadiz, for Castine, sprung a leak, and was abandoned 20th Oct; the crew were picked up the next day in their boats, by brig Ottoman, at Boston, from Malaga. The ship sunk in 12 hours after she was abandoned.*[35]

Fortunately, the captain and crew were saved but the *St. Leon* was gone, surrendering her cargo of salt back to the sea.

---

34. Wayne M. O'Leary, "The Maine Transatlantic Salt Trade in the Nineteenth Century," *The American Neptune*, vol. 47, No. 2, (1987), 100.

35. *The Sailor's Magazine*, vol. 24–25, American Seamen's Friend Society, (1852), 524.

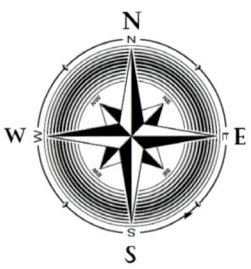

Ship *Adams*: Family Matters

Glass model of the ship *Adams*. Courtesy Wilson Museum. The *Adams* was built at Castine in 1840 and was 592 tons with dimensions of 143'x31'x15'. She was owned by Samuel Adams, Benjamin D. Gay, Thomas Cobb, Robert Perkins, et al., Castine.

The ship *Adams* was a well-documented participant in the Castine triangle trade route, completing it seven times during the years 1842 and 1849 with Moses Gay as Master.[36]

36. Wayne M. O'Leary, "The Maine Transatlantic Salt Trade in the Nineteenth Century," *The American Neptune*, vol. 47, No. 2, (1987), 92.

Captain Moses Gay was the ninth and youngest child of Moses Gay and Phebe Perkins Gay, who built the house overlooking the harbor on the embankment between Green and Dyer Streets after their marriage in 1795. Born in Castine in 1815, Captain Gay started his sailing career at the age of 16 as a cabin boy on the ship *Canova* under the watchful eye of Captain Henry Whitney.[37] In 1841 at the age of 26, Moses married Captain Whitney's daughter Lucy and took command of his first ship, the Castine built *Adams*.

Marriage to a ship captain was a lonely life. Castine-based ship captains were typically away at sea for ten or eleven months at a time before returning home late in the year for a few short weeks with their families. This way of life posed a difficult dilemma—travel together with the family and be exposed to the difficulties and risks of a life at sea or tolerate being separated for most of the year until the ship returned to home port.

During long voyages, hand-written letters were the only means of communication between those at sea and those eagerly awaiting news from their loved ones at home. Whether sent from domestic or foreign ports, letters traveled by sea to their ultimate destination, and it was often months before these letters were finally received—and some were never delivered.

After her marriage to Captain Moses Gay in 1841, Lucy Whitney Gay remained at home in Castine and endured five years of lengthy periods of separation from her husband. In the spring of 1846 Lucy decided to join her husband at sea on the ship *Adams*, even though her health was poor.

The following letter, from Captain Moses Gay and Lucy, was written during their first voyage together in 1846. The letter was sent from the cotton port of Charleston, South Carolina, to Lucy's mother and sister Frances in Castine, who eagerly awaited news of Lucy's new life at sea:

Scale drawing of sparring plan for ship *Adams*, c. 1840. Copy photo courtesy of Castine Historical Society.

Charleston S. C. April 19, 1846

Dear Mother Whitney, I presume you have been expecting letters some time from Lucy or myself, and I have been waiting for Lucy to commence, but find it is no use—for she likes to take her time, but I presume she has a good excuse for her head has been quite bad since our arrival, and she has been bled within a few days which has done her good. Lucy is very well indeed at sea, and enjoys it very well, and as for sea-sickness, she hardly knows what it is, and I often tell her that she should be so a little more to be genteel. It is quite strange that her old feelings return as soon as we get into Port, and when at sea she does not feel them. It is uncertain where we shall go from here—and I am now waiting for letters from Castine which I hope will give me some instructions so that I can make up my mind what to do. I soon expect to go to New Orleans from here, as business at this place is very

---

37. *Lewiston Evening Journal*, September 10, 1943, p. 4.

dull indeed nothing of consequence doing. If we should go there it will be rather late in the Fall before we see you, but it will be the more pleasant—Lucy will write you and Sister Franz[38] a few lines in this, so I will leave her a good lot of room. Hoping this will find you and all the family well—I remain

Your affectionate son,
Moses Gay
Monday morning, April 20

Lucy Whitney Gay continues writing in the same letter to her sister Frances:

Dear Sister Frances,

As Moses has written his part of the letter to Mother, I will fill up the remainder to you and answer your long and interesting letter which I received a few days since. I intended answering it immediately after receiving it but my head would not allow of it and indeed today I am hardly in a writing mood but I thought you would expect an answer to your letter long ere this. I wrote you from Liverpool—did you receive the letter? —you did not write anything about it in your letter.

I suppose you think by this time I can tell you just how I like going to sea, I like it very much and feel much better than I do on shore, although we have experienced some very severe weather, but I did not suffer from sea sickness, nor the big seas did not frighten me so of course I enjoyed myself very well; I should lik't to have had Mother with me although I think she would not have enjoyed it much with her courage.

We next learn of Lucy's impressions of Charleston, her thoughts about the inability to have children, and her younger sister Frances' budding relationship with ship captain Leonard Whiting:

I suppose you would like to know how I am pleased with Charleston. I like it pretty well. I should think it a very quiet orderly city. I have been out a number of times and have enjoyed myself very much but now and then my head disturbs me a little as usual at this season which is not quite as pleasant but on the whole I think it a little better than when I left home, but I could not get along without being bled; I have felt better since or imagined myself so.

I cannot tell you how long we shall remain here it is quite uncertain, perhaps we shall go to N Orleans and would you not pity me with the hot weather and

Meeting Street, Charleston, South Carolina,
Illustration from *Frank Leslie's Illustrated Newspaper*, 1861. Courtesy National Park Service.

moschetoes to contend with, would you like to be in my place? I think it will be quite late in the fall before I shall have the pleasure of seeing you all again, you say in your letter you suppose you must wait until that time before you see me, unless! ------------. I am quite free from anything of that kind at present, and more than that, always expect to be. When you get married you must have my number for me, and is the knot to be tied before we

---

38. Franz is the nickname for Frances Whitney.

get home? I hope not, I suppose you have decided upon that ere this write and tell me all about it. I suppose you are anticipating a great deal in welcoming your Leonard home, I hope you will realize all; if we go to N. O. I hope we shall not find him gone; Frances I think you will find in him a good husband and he will do everything in his power to make you happy but I suppose you are well aware of that already you know his worth perhaps far better than I do.

John William Hill, *Bird's Eye View of Charleston,* (London: Smith Brothers & Co., 1851). Courtesy Historic Charleston Foundation, Charleston, South Carolina.

The longing for news from home was ever-present and letters, carried by merchant ships to intercept the recipients at far off ports, were often missed. Lucy continues writing to her sister Frances:

I found it quite a treat to get your letter of news after being at sea so long and hope soon I shall receive just such another one, has not Phebe learned to write a letter yet? I should think Lucy Ann, Phebe would write me, and tell me all about their examination if they got through without fainting.

You say in your letter you suppose your letters were received in Liverpool, I got one but there is one I have still to receive, one which you wrote to N. O. I have not got; you write me about purchasing you a silk dress in Liverpool, all silks are very dear there, you cannot get a handsome dress for less than 18 or $20, are you willing I should give that price for it?

The weather is not very warm here now. There are a number of ladies who called on me since I have been here and some very pleasant. I am much pleased with all those I have seen. Don't forget to write me again while I am here for I hate to be disappointed if you do not write all the news for I am just as curious as ever to hear.

One advantage of going to sea was the ability to meet up with family and friends in faraway ports. Lucy mentions meeting up with two of her brothers, Henry and Sam, while in New Orleans. Lucy also mentions the difficulty and loneliness of captains being separated from their wives:

I suppose it is quite uncertain when brother Henry is home again; I should think Mother would miss him very much. He appeared in good spirits when at N. O. he often dined with me and brother Sam also. You wrote me in one of your letters about Mrs. Wescotts going to sea next fall. I think it would add greatly to her husband's happiness if she did go, for he looked rather sad when I saw him in Liverpool. I boarded at the same house with him.

Lucy's letter closes with a brief message from Moses mentioning crossing off, which was a practice of writing both horizontally and vertically on the same page to conserve paper:

Dear Sis. Lucy has written so much that I have not much for a postscript—and you know I hate crossing off so you must take the will for the deed. Yours as ever, Moses.[39]

Lucy and Moses' life together at sea was cut short several months after this letter was written when Lucy contracted smallpox and died in Le Havre, France in 1847. Captain Moses remained a close friend of the Whitney family and eventually married Lucy Ann Adams, Lucy Whitney's niece.

Frances Whitney, another of Henry Whitney's daughters, married Leonard Jarvis Whiting, shortly after Lucy's death in 1847. Captain Whiting was a native of Surry, Maine and was based out of the cotton trading port of New Orleans. Frances most likely accompanied her husband at sea until she became pregnant. She then moved into lodgings in Algiers, a town located just across the Mississippi River from the bustling port of New Orleans, to await the birth of her first child. John Perkins Whiting was born in New Orleans in 1848 and Frances remained on shore, missing her husband and her family back in Castine.

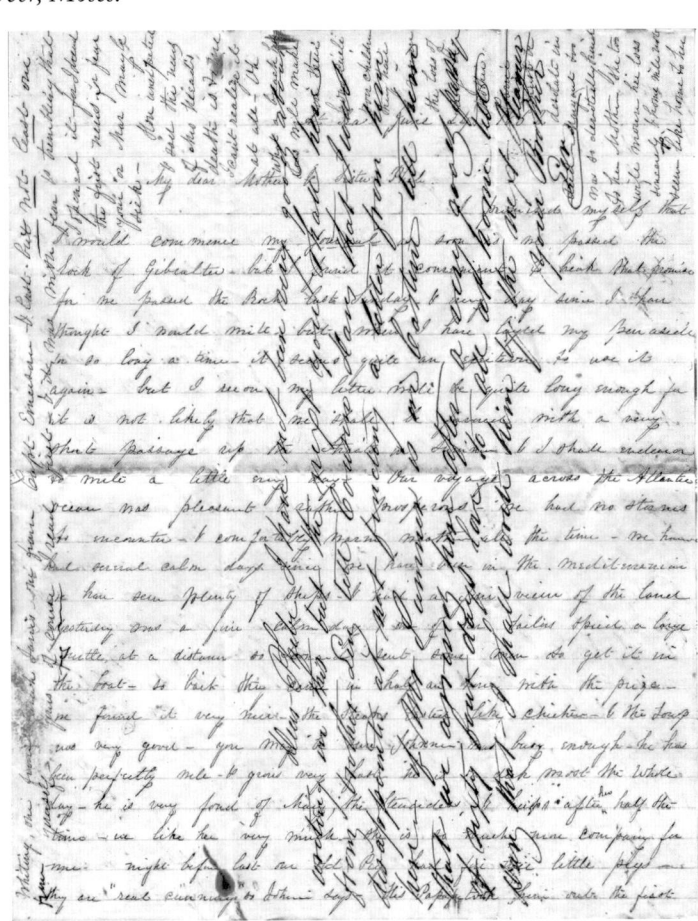

Example of "crossing off" in letter writing at sea.
Courtesy Castine Historical Society.

I fancied that I were home —with you all in our snug little sitting-room—but oh! my how far I am from you. I wonder sometimes how I can keep away from home so long—when I used to be such a home-body—but after one is married they must be content to remain where it is fa [sic for] the husbands interests—and I am so, fa I have got one of the best husbands in the world.[40]

---

39. Letter from Captain Moses Gay and Lucy Whitney Gay to her mother and sister, April 20, 1846. Castine Historical Society.

40. Letter from Frances Whitney Whiting to her mother, niece and sister, December 22, 1848. Castine Historical Society.

Frances was not entirely alone in New Orleans. Her brother, Samuel Whitney, lived there as did several of her relatives and friends from Castine. In addition, ships from Castine were regular visitors to the New Orleans port, bringing welcomed visitors, letters and news from home.

J. Bachmann, detail of *Birds' Eye View of New Orleans,* c. 1851. (New York: A. Guerber & Co.,). Courtesy Library of Congress, Washington D.C.

In a letter from Castine visitor Thomas Brown Hooke, we learn that Frances and her newborn son are boarding with her first cousin, Phebe Perkins Whitney Hooke:

Elisha just called![41] Captain Whiting left last night. His wife and little boy board with Phebe this winter. The Capt. left in haste last eve and E. came over to see how his wife was and bring a note from him. She feels like all wives—poor thing—would like to go with him but the little John Perkins Whitney Whiting (a long name) is but two weeks old and the Capt. thinks he is to young to go to sea. Phebe is quite happy to have her with her. [42]

The hot and humid climate of New Orleans combined with poor sanitary conditions rendered the city ripe for the spread of disease. Frances writes home describing a cholera outbreak that paralyzed the Crescent City starting in December 1848. Up to one hundred people were dying a day and like many other inhabitants Frances considers leaving New Orleans to protect herself and her young son from this virulent epidemic:

You probably have heard that the cholera is in town—and prevailing to a considerable extent. I feel unpleasant about it—there are very sudden deaths every day—& the Physicians pronounce it to be an epidemic—it is

---

41. Elisha Dyer is the brother of Hannah Dyer. Captain Leonard Jarvis Whiting is the husband of Frances Whitney Whiting.

42. Letter from Thomas Brown Hooke to his wife, Hannah Dyer, from Belleville (across the river from New Orleans), October 31, 1848. Transcript at Castine Historical Society.

such a dreadful disease—persons die so suddenly—we have had such unusually warm weather fa [sic] two weeks —so unfavorable fa it—the Doct's think as soon as the weather changes & becomes cool that the disease will be checked. I sincerely hope so—it has been uncomfortably warm. I have been dressed in summer clothing & have <u>suffered with heat in Dec.</u>—have not had a fan in my room fa all a week & had the doors & windows open. I was hoping that I might go over to town today to buy some Christmas presents to send home by Jeff Whiting who goes with Capt. Emerson in a day or two. I wanted to get a present fa Johnny to send his grandma—she has been so kind as to send him a blanket to keep him warm. I dare not go over now while it is so sickly—not wishing to run any risk—many are leaving the city. I told Capt. Emerson I believed I would take passage with him to Boston he said he would take me—he would have to take Sarah & the baby too—but I <u>don't</u> think that will do.

Frances was very eager to join her husband again at sea and Captain Leonard Whiting was busily making on-board preparations for accommodating his growing family:

"I received a letter from him [Leonard] Friday—the poor fellow had a long passage and when he wrote he was not in the Antwerp but was detained in Portsmouth by a head wind for seven days & from there he sent my letter—it was too bad—I cannot now expect him until the second week in March—but that will soon be here—he writes me that he has been very lonely this passage—but has busied himself in altering and enlarging our stateroom—and lots of other fixins—but almost the whole letter was about his boy. I could not help laughing—he will expect to see the child walking when he comes I have no doubt.[43]

H. W. Hoogkamer, *The Devil's Tongue*, mid-19th century print of the Rock of Gibraltar. Unknown source.

Frances did return to sea with her husband and young son Johnny. The next we hear from her is in 1852 at sea on the ship *European* on a voyage from Apalachicola, Florida to the Adriatic seaport of Trieste. Their cargo was most likely cotton and the voyage lasted 64 days. The letter provides interesting insights into life at sea with a family during the 1850s. During this voyage, the proud parents commissioned a portrait of their four-year-old son John by an Italian artist. When this letter was written, Frances was two months pregnant with her second child, who would be born in Liverpool on January 16th, 1853 and named Annie Thorburn Whiting:

At Sea, June 24, 1852

My dear Mother and Sister Phebe.

I promised myself that I would commence my journal as soon as we passed the Rock of Gibraltar, but I found it convenient to break that promise for we passed the Rock last Sunday & every day since I have thought I would write—but when I have layed[sic] my pen aside in so long a time it seems quite an exertion to use it again—but

---

43. Letter from Frances Whitney Whiting to her sister Phebe Whitney and cousin Lucy Ann Adams, February 11, 1849. Castine Historical Society.

I recon[sic] my letter will be quite long enough fa it is not likely that we shall be favored with a very short passage up the Straits in summer & I shall endeavor to write a little every day.

In the writings below, we learn about some of the food sources available during voyages and how people kept themselves busy during periods of calm sailing:

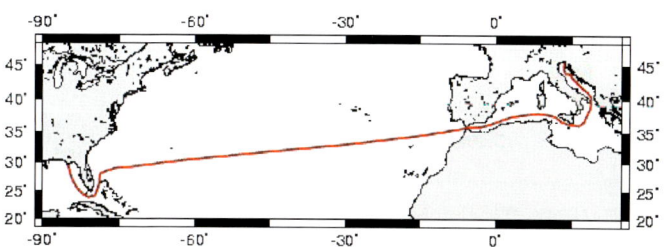

Route from Apalachicola, Florida to Trieste.

Our voyage across the Atlantic Ocean was pleasant & rather prosperous—we had no storms to encounter & comfortably warm weather all the time—we have had several calm days since we have been in the Mediterranean & have seen plenty of ships—& had a fine view of the land. Yesterday was a fine calm day & one of our sailors spied a large turtle, at a distance so Leonard sent some men to get it in the boat—so they came in half an hour with the prize—we found it very nice—the steaks tasted like chicken - & the soup was very good— you may be sure Johnnie was busy enough—he has been perfectly well & grows very fast—he is on deck most of the whole day—he is very fond of Mary, the Stewardess, & keeps after her half the time—we like her very much. She is so much more company fa me.

Night before last our old pig had five little pigs—they are "real cunning" so Johnnie says —His Papa took him out the first thing in the morning—he was perfectly wild with delight—he had many questions to ask about

Unknown artist, *Portrait of John Perkins Whiting*, 1852. Painted while on a voyage with his parents. Private Collection.

them, where they came from etc. etc.. We are quite fortunate to have them all live. Johnnie says that I must tell you that "his hen lays him an egg every day in the shop."

Leonard was very busy last week making a bird cage and it is really a fine one, wish you could see it. The canary likes it much. This week he has amused himself with making some very pretty "joggle sticks," [44] *they are fa us, to beat him in playing this winter. You remember I dare say how he used to cheat & for two or three days he has been making little boxes for my spools. Johnnie is of course the busiest one on the ship. He says, "if Mr. Cavel in Trieste asks him who he is—he shall just tell him that he is Mr. Whiting the third mate." Don't you think that he is coming on the stage fast!*

---

44. Joggle sticks were used for a game similar to the game of pick up sticks.

As the letter continues, we find the ship *European* has rounded the heel of the boot of Italy and is sailing northwest towards its destination of Trieste. We learn of the welcomed crossing paths with other ships at sea and get a glimpse of seafaring competitiveness:

I am happy to tell you that we are now in the Adriatic Sea, We have had a noble wind & are nearing our destined port & if we could be favored with a good wind for these days we would be in Trieste. We had the pleasure of talking with an American Captain yesterday—our ships were very near together—his wife & little boy about as large as Johnnie were with him also the Mates wife—it was very pleasant to have company at sea—they are bound to Trieste—but we have the satisfaction of being a little ahead of them, they left Apalachicola several days before we did—there is also an American Bark in company with us bound to Trieste that left N. O. sometime before we did. Johnnie was delighted to see the little boy yesterday he began to show off by pulling the ropes.

As the final destination becomes closer, one can detect impatience after a long journey and eager anticipation of receiving letters with news from home:

Monday 12ᵗʰ

Since I wrote we have been beating about with a head wind, making but little progress towards our desired port, which makes us more impatient fa we are only one hundred & fifty miles from there - & a fair wind would very soon take us there. We have been very near some pretty islands—they all look familiar to me—having passed these before.

I long to hear from you—I sincerely hope Ma will be well this summer. I dread the summer months for her. I want to hear from poor Nancy's family[45]—what a desolate place it must be there—I fear that the family cannot be kept together a great while longer & I should hate to have them scattered. I hope the child you have will prove to be a good obedient one & from Lucy Ann I want to hear where she is etc. etc. Your letters will tell me all—oh how I want to get them. I am getting impatient—more again bye & bye.

Wednesday 14ᵗʰ.

Yesterday we had the pleasure of welcoming a pilot on board— a rough old looking Italian. Johnnie looked at him with astonishment - & got all his things to show him.

Finally, after a journey of sixty-four days at sea, the *European* arrives at Trieste with a promise of fresh fruit and anxiousness about the long-anticipated news from home:

Sunday Morning, 18ᵗʰ

We arrived in Trieste last eve. I am happy to say—fa [sic] the last three days it has been almost calm. We think our passage a fair one. The city looks beautifully. The mountains are a perfect garden. Leonard has gone to the health office & took Johnnie with him. He was delighted to be dressed once more & the way he strutted about the deck would have amused you. I only hope Leonard will bring my letters—but I fear not fa he can't go anywhere until the officer comes off with him to count the men. I hope to have some fruit—they say there is an abundance here. Leonard has just come with the letters—which were most welcome & Johnnie with an immense bouquet of

---

45. Nancy Whitney Adams, Frances' eldest sister, who died in January 1852, leaving twelve children behind.

beautiful flowers—one letter from Mother Whiting, one from Sarah Jarvis, one from Capt. Emerson & last but not least, one from yourself. Yours of course I read first—& it was with fear & trembling that I opened it—for I dread the first news for fear you or Ma maybe sick.[46]

Frances remained at sea on the ship *European* with her husband and young son until their daughter, Annie T. Whiting, was born in Liverpool in January of 1853. A letter from Leonard to his mother tells us that Frances waited only three weeks before returning to sea—she was no doubt eager to return to Castine to show off her new baby:

Boston, Feb 23, 1853

Dear Mother

You will be glad to hear of our safe arrival here. Franz[47] *& the baby are first rate. We arrived on Saturday & went to the hotel. In the afternoon, Uncle James & his wife came down & made us pack up &*

Frances Whitney Whiting and John Perkins Whiting, 1852. On board ship. Courtesy Castine Historical Society.

View of Trieste, 1850. A. D. Gregorio/De Agosini/Getty Images.

---

46. Letter from Frances Whitney Whiting to her mother and sister. Castine Historical Society.

47. Franz is the nickname for Leonard Whiting's wife, Frances Whitney Whiting.

go to their house. I have not yet recovered my strength but am much better than when I left Liverpool. We called on Mary Jane on Monday - found her in good spirits & she & Mrs Wilson thought that Franz was pretty smart to come from Liverpool with the child only three weeks old. We shall start for Castine tomorrow. I can not tell how long before I shall get away until I arrive at Castine as I do not know how far the ship[48] is along.[49]

Soon after arriving safely home in Castine from this Mediterranean voyage, Leonard Whiting took command of the newly launched Castine ship *J. P. Whitney* - and his growing family was forced to confront the confounded Captain's family dilemma—head out to sea together or live separated lives.

The ship *Adams* remained as part of the Castine fleet until she was sold to Liverpool owners in 1863. She remained in service until 1872 having a full life at sea of 23 years.

---

48. Ship *J. P. Whitney*, which was being built in Castine and would be Captain Leonard Whiting's next command.

49. Letter from Leonard Jarvis Whiting to his mother, Sarah Jarvis Whiting. Castine Historical Society.

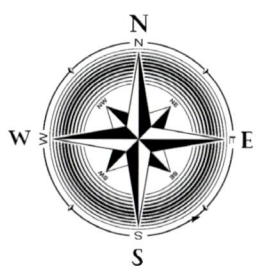

Ship *William Jarvis*: A Rough Voyage and Perils of African American Crews

Unknown artist, ship *William Jarvis*. Private Collection. Here shown leaving Leghorn (Livorno, Italy) bound for New York in 1855, Master William Ballard. The Marryat Code hoist on the mizzen head correctly reads 6,1,3,7 under the 2nd distinguishing pennant. Built at Castine in 1848 by Samuel Noyes, she was 667 tons with dimensions of 142' x 32' x 16'. Owners were John H. Jarvis, William Jarvis, John H. Jarvis, Jr., Frederick A. Jarvis and Isaiah Wescott of Castine.

The Irish potato famine, between 1845 and 1852, was a time of dramatically increased demand for ships to transport emigrants from Ireland and England to the United States.[50] Carrying passengers

---

50. *The Illustrated London News*, July 6, 1850.

was quite profitable and ships specifically designed for carrying human freight could demand higher rates. The Castine ship *William Jarvis*, launched in 1848, boasted specific features to make her more attractive for carrying passengers including, "the provision made for securing the thorough ventilation of the whole vessel - thereby promoting the health of passengers and crew."[51]

Before 1849 the usual practice was for ships to wait at port until they were fully loaded before departing. The amount of time to secure passengers and freight, and complete the loading process, was unpredictable. To meet the increasing emigrant demand from European ports several competing "Packet Lines" with regularly scheduled sailings were organized. The *William Jarvis* participated in this packet trade and sailed for the Black Star Line between Liverpool and New York in 1849, the Train & Company Line between Liverpool and Boston in 1851 and the coastal Brigham Line in 1854 and 1857.[52]

William Lighton's account of the teeming Liverpool docks and a rough autumn voyage on the *William Jarvis* from Liverpool to Boston describes some of the perils experienced by packet ship passengers:

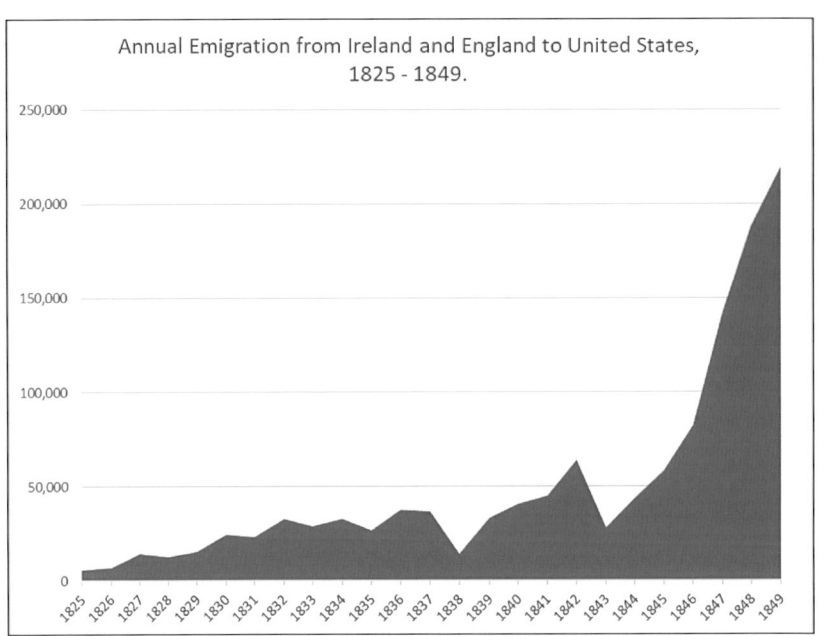

Number of emigrants from Ireland and England to the United States, 1825-1849. Data from *The Illustrated London News*, July 6, 1850.

We arrived at Liverpool about three o'clock, and proceeded at once to secure our passage on board the ship, William Jarvis, commander William Jarvis, to Boston, to sail in three days.

Liverpool in many parts presented a sorrowful appearance— it was England and Ireland combined, the inhabitants of the latter country having collected in thousands on the docks for emigration, and other purposes. It is a pitiable sight to see such swarms of oppressed sufferers forsaking old homes, friends, and interests, to seek abroad immunity from the grinding power of despotism.

If you wish to see street life in the vicinity of the docks, you must view it in the evening, first taking the precaution to put on a resolute purpose, and dignity of manner, or the unwary is apt to be enticed by the base and vicious to ruin. Multitudes of men and women degraded to the lowest conceivable condition, throng the way, whilst sinks of crime fester on every hand, epitomes of perdition. Interspersed are individuals and families soliciting charity; with the poor pale faced children from the infant to the child of twelve years old ranged in a row, imploring in piteous silence the generosity of passers by. Such touching scenes are wont to raise the head to look up to a God of mercy, for how few compared with their ability pay any regard to the misfortunes of their fellow creatures.

51. Marine List, *Republican Journal*, (Belfast, Maine) 24 August 1848.

52. Carl C. Cutler, *Queens of the Western Ocean*, (Annapolis: The United States Naval Institute, 1961), 372, 384, 524, 525.

After surviving the chaotic and miserable Liverpool dock scene, the passengers of the *William Jarvis* were ready for sea. But there was another example of deception to be uncovered before their final departure:

Saturday, September 1st, the ship cleared out of dock, to wait the morning tide in a more spacious berth, and the next day when the bells were chiming for worship a steam tug towed us into the channel, far from the old loved isle.

From the day we secured our passage, we were much annoyed by the airs of a young man, who insisted by priority on the cabin we had paid the captain for. But on investigation it was found he had no business in the ship, as his passage money had not been received, and he was politely landed ashore in the tug.

Like many others he had been cheated by an unprincipled runner, and probably before he hires a passage again, will know who he pays.

At sea, many were afflicted by sea-sickness and there was always the threat of storms and violent weather to make the passage miserable. Those wealthy enough to afford cabin berths had it much better than the unfortunate souls confined to the crowded steerage deck below:

When freed from the steamer, and at the mercy of the winds and waves, the sails were spread, and we sped away on the broad deep ocean. My terrible foe soon reduced me to a state of apathy, but my companion buoyant with hope thought himself invulnerable; however, Neptune was not to be balked, and suddenly arrested him when about to attack an excellent dinner.

Our cabin was a nice little apartment on deck, where I had power to appreciate the glories displayed by the Almighty in the heavens and on the deep. I had, besides, a collection of the favorite songsters of my boyhood, which cheered me with their melody.

THE DEPARTURE.

The Departure, from *The Illustrated London News*, July 6, 1850.
Courtesy Illustrated London News Ltd/Mary Evans.

The 12th the sea was high and violent, and the ship rolled and pitched as if contending for the right of mastery with the raging main. The main top mast, yielding before the blast, broke, and caused great consternation among the passengers, who feared the vessel was about to flounder. In spite of the storm, the crew toiled bravely until every part was repaired, but alas, it soon snapped again amid the mad war of elements, and then arose the impotent rage of man, for the sailors raved and swore as if they thought oaths would control the tempest. Again was the mast replaced with better success, the crew working as if the storm had no power to alarm, nor the rocking of the ship to incommode them.

During the intense excitement among the passengers, a poor woman was robbed of her money and other valuables; another who was most ardent in her devotions in the time of danger, I heard swearing, a few hours after, because she could not cook her supper.

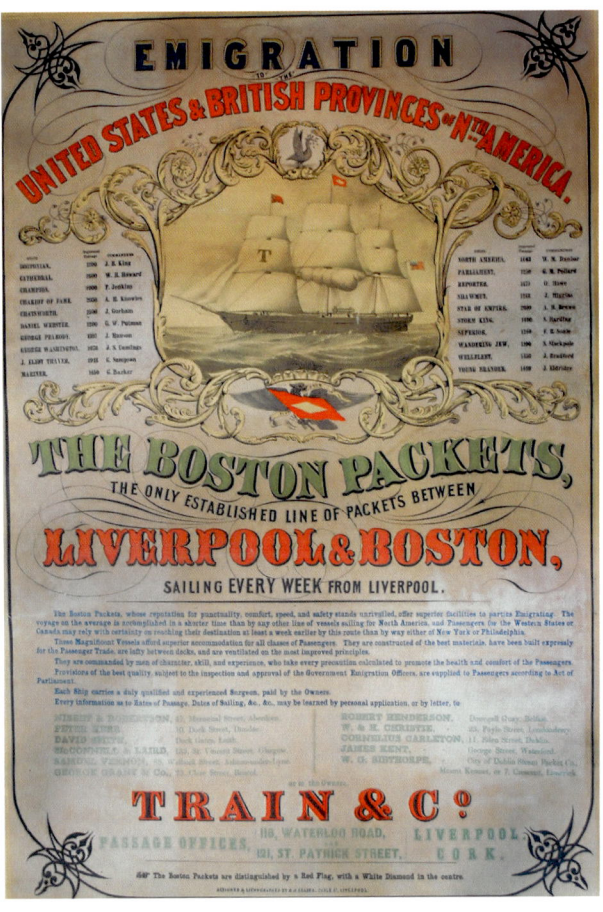

Train & Co., Boston Packets advertisement, 1855. Courtesy Bostonian Society, Boston, Massachusetts.

It was amusing to watch the gyrations performed by things animate and inanimate, in their efforts to gain the cook house, which if reached would be sometimes deluged with a heavy sea that capsized all in it. A jolly, well conditioned son of Erin was often the subject of much sport, for he would fall on the deck slap dash like a flounder, and before he could recover his footing, another heave pitched him over again, to the outpouring of some Irish spirit. Several were severely burned, and a young lady had her foot badly scaled by putting it in a pot of boilin gruel a boy had set down on the deck.

Rather than abating, the raging storms continued. One can only imagine the suffering and despair endured by the passengers, most of whom had never been at sea:

Wednesday, 19th, the equinoctial gale commenced, and increased to a storm, which again broke our top mast. The ocean presented a wild and terrifying aspect, and especially, during the night, a sublimity that baffled description. It was one mighty, unbroken expanse of seething water as far as the eye could scan, and seemed as if old Ocean convulsed with madness was turning his lowest depths to the sky.

To me, nothing exhibits the majesty and power of God so much as a storm at sea, when the heavens are robed in darkness and not a star cheers the heart of the mariner—the wind howling and shaking for her destruction. At such a time, but for belief in the almighty goodness, one's "heart and flesh would utterly fail:" this knowledge is as oil to the troubled spirit, and sustains the soul ready to die.

By this continuance of foul weather, I became almost helpless from severe sickness, so that I had enough to do to prevent myself being stove to death, and it was with a feeling of humble gratitude, shared in by all that the sight of land was hailed.

On Saturday, 29th, at 2 o'clock P. M. we anchored at the quarantine and all save one passed the customary inspection.[53]

After a perilous voyage across the Atlantic of twenty-nine days, the *William Jarvis* arrived safely in Boston and dispatched its weary passengers, who were delighted to be on terra firma once more.

Another event recorded during the life of the *William Jarvis* is an 1859 court case heard in Massachusetts. The case involved an African American crew who complained, that after arriving in New Orleans from Le Havre, they were forced to sail to Boston rather than being released in New Orleans.

Free men of color started working on sailing vessels after the American Revolution. In addition to being sailors, the positions of cook and steward were commonly held by African Americans. A life at sea offered these men a decent pay, but they were viewed with suspicion at southern ports where slavery was still active.

In Charleston during the summer of 1822 a free black man and ex-sailor, Denmark Vesey, was suspected of planning a slave rebellion. Vesey and his followers were accused of planning to kill slaveholders in Charleston, liberate their slaves, and sail to the black republic of Haiti for

OFFICIAL REPORT

OF THE

TRIALS OF SUNDRY NEGROES,

CHARGED

WITH AN ATTEMPT TO RAISE

AN INSURRECTION

IN THE STATE OF SOUTH-CAROLINA:

PRECEDED BY AN

INTRODUCTION AND NARRATIVE;

AND

IN AN APPENDIX,

A REPORT OF THE TRIALS OF

FOUR WHITE PERSONS,

ON INDICTMENTS FOR ATTEMPTING TO EXCITE THE SLAVES TO INSURRECTION.

Prepared and Published at the request of the Court.

By LIONEL H. KENNEDY & THOMAS PARKER,
Members of the Charleston Bar, and the Presiding Magistrates of the Court.

CHARLESTON:
PRINTED BY JAMES R. SCHENCK, 23, BROAD-STREET.
1822.

Report on attempted Charleston insurrection. (Charleston: James R. Schenck, 1822), Courtesy Library of Congress, Washington D.C.

refuge. Word of the plan was leaked, and city officials ordered a militia to arrest the plot's leaders and suspected followers before the uprising could begin. A city-appointed court convicted sixty-seven blacks of trying to raise an insurrection and thirty-five, including Vesey, were hanged.

It was feared that this planned rebellion was encouraged by free black sailors spreading ideas gained from northern and foreign ports where slavery no longer existed. In response to these fears, South Carolina passed the "Act for the Better Regulation and Government of Free Negroes and Persons of Color" in December of 1822. This law stipulated *"if any vessel shall come into any port or harbor of this State ... having on board any free negroes or persons of color as cooks, stewards, mariners, or in any other employment on board of said vessel, such free negroes or persons of color shall be ... confined in jail until said vessel shall clear out and depart from this state."*

---

53. *Autobiography and Reminiscences of William Beebey Lighton*, (Albany: Munsell, 1854), 305–308.

It went on to say if the ship's captain did not remove his free black sailors or pay expenses for their detention, they would be considered slaves and would be sold.[54]

The states of Georgia, North Carolina, Alabama and Louisiana passed similar Negro Seamen Acts during the 1830s and 1840s. Under these laws jail expenses for free black sailors at southern ports became a considerable burden for ship owners who were liable for these costs. In the Louisiana version of the law, starting in 1852, black sailors were allowed to remain on board, but the captain of the ship was required to guarantee that they would be taken out of the state. Evidence of enforcement of this law can be found in New Orleans police records that show that arrests of free blacks in the city peaked between 1859 and 1862.[55]

The ship *William Jarvis* arrived at Boston in May 1859 with a disgruntled African American crew. In their complaint, the crew stated that the voyage described in the shipping articles was from "Havre to New Orleans, and thence to one or more ports in Europe, and finally back to a port of discharge in the United States, for a period not exceeding twelve calendar months."

Upon arrival in New Orleans, cargo shipped from Le Havre was unloaded and instead of sailing to another European port, the *William Jarvis* sailed to Boston. Since no second voyage to Europe was made, the crew argued that arrival in New Orleans should have ended their contract allowing them to be released. However, their request for release was refused by the captain and they were forced to sail to Boston without a contract.

Captain Ballard, master of the *William Jarvis*, argued that he was acting in accordance with the Louisiana Negro Seamen Act, which prohibited him from releasing his crew of free black sailors in New Orleans and required him to guarantee that they be taken out of state.

After hearing details of the case, the Massachusetts judge ruled that specific language of the shipping articles did not require the crew to sail to Boston and that the Louisiana law requiring the black sailors to be taken out of state was inconsistent with the constitution and laws of the United States. He ruled in favor of the crew and the ship's owners were ordered to pay $383.82 and costs.[56]

The ship *William Jarvis* had a good life of twelve years primarily trading between east coast ports of the United States and Europe. The following account of her 1860 demise on Marquis Key, Florida, was reported from Key West:

In the absence of the United States Judge for this District, the case of the wrecked ship Wm. Jarvis has been settled by mutual agreement between the parties interested—the salvors to receive the sum of $9500 for services rendered by them in saving cargo and materials. The damaged portion of the cargo and materials have been sold, bringing $6200; the dry portion will be reshipped to its destination.[57]

---

54. W. Jeffrey Bolster, *Black Jacks, African American Seamen in the Age of Sail*, (Cambridge: Harvard University Press, 1997), 218.

55. Ibid., 230

56. *Decisions of Hon. Peleg Sprague, in Admiralty and Maritime Causes in The District Court of the United States for The District of Massachusetts*, vol. 1, (Philadelphia: T & J. W. Johnson & Co., 1861).

57. *The Times Picayune*, Friday October 19, 1860.

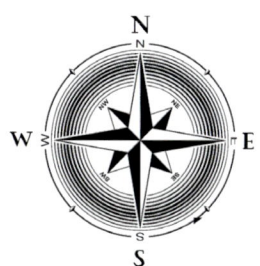

Ship *William Witherle*: Demise of the American Merchant Fleet

Unknown artist, ship *William Witherle*. Courtesy Witherle Memorial Library, Castine, Maine. Here shown in two views off the South Stack, Anglesey, North Wales. Built at Castine in 1851 by Samuel Noyes for a cost of $46,787, she was 874 tons with dimensions of 162' x 34' x 17'. Owners were William Witherle, 3/8; Isaiah Wescott, 1/8; Joseph Wescott, 1/8; David L. Stevens, 1/8; Charles Atherton, 1/16; Hezekiah Williams, 1/16; Samuel Noyes, 1/24; Joshua H. Noyes, 1/24; and Samuel T. Noyes, 1/24; of Castine.

The *William Witherle* was named after a successful Castine merchant and ship owner who thrived in numerous business partnerships between 1806 and 1855. He owned a store along the waterfront and one of the largest wharfs at the foot of Green Street.

Witherle & Co. and Adams & Co. storefronts, c. 1855. Courtesy Wilson Museum, Castine, Maine.

The onset of the Civil War resulted in irreparable damage to the dominance of American shipping as both Union and Confederate actions were taken to prevent cotton exports. The Union understood that cotton exports were the driving force for the economy of the Confederate states, and to constrict this critical source of income the Union navy implemented General Scott's "Great Snake" which blockaded and choked off southern ports.

Southern planters and cotton merchants, who understood that the textile industries of Britain and France depended on regular supplies of reasonably priced American cotton, believed that driving up cotton prices would cause European intervention in the war. In what became known as "cotton diplomacy", the Confederate states choked off supplies of cotton with an embargo.

The pain was immediately felt by the manufacturers in Britain and France who lobbied their respective governments to recognize the Confederacy to restore the flow of cotton. However, Britain and France were determined to remain neutral and successfully replaced American cotton with imports from East Indian and Egyptian sources thereby foiling the Confederate's plans.

An important element of the Confederate naval strategy was to disrupt Union maritime commerce. To pursue this goal, the Confederates commissioned fast steam and sail powered "cruisers" which were secretly built in Britain. These vessels were designed to be fast enough to avoid Union warships while carrying enough firepower to capture unarmed merchant ships.

The Confederate cruisers patrolled international shipping lanes and were successful in capturing and destroying some 200 merchant vessels, which was rather insignificant when compared to the total num-

G. Perkins, *Destruction of the Clipper Ship Jacob Bell by the British Pirate Florida*, from *Harper's Weekly*, January-June 1863. Courtesy Hampton Roads Naval Museum, Norfolk, Virginia.

ber of American vessels at sea. A more menacing result of these cruisers' raids was a punishing increase in insurance premiums for all American-flagged ships.

One such insurance component was the war premium for freight, which peaked at 9% in 1863. This meant that for every $100 of cargo shipped on an American vessel the owner of the freight would have to pay $9 above the regular marine insurance rate. To remain competitive with foreign vessels, American ship owners were forced to reduce their freight charges. In addition to war premiums for freight, American owners also had to pay significantly increased rates of insurance for the vessel itself to cover the higher risk of being captured and burned by Confederate raiders. The combination of

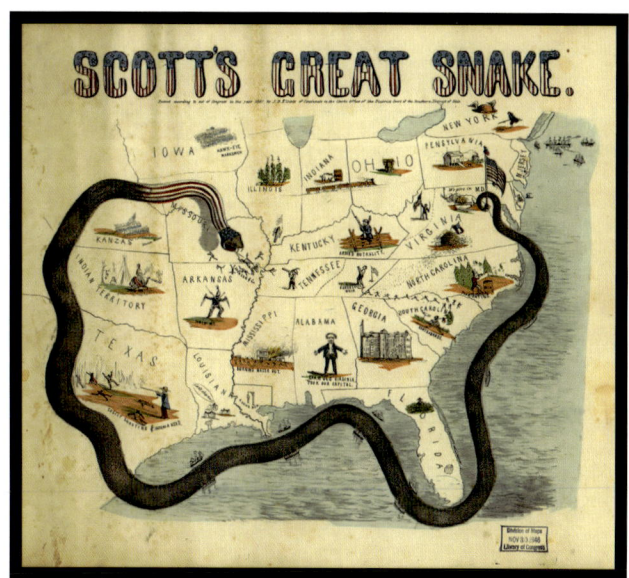

Scott's Great Snake. Entered according to Act of Congress in the year, 1861. Courtesy Library of Congress, Washington D.C.

these increases resulted in neutral vessels having a 25% cost advantage over their American counterparts. These circumstances encouraged owners of American ships to sell them abroad. Between 1860 and 1864 more than 1000 vessels, which represented more than half of the entire American fleet, were sold to foreign owners. Those that remained under the American flag tended to be older and less attractive to foreign buyers.[58]

The *William Witherle* was sold to German interests in 1864 and renamed *Selma*. She sailed out of the port of Altona (Hamburg), Germany and was last listed there in the *Lloyd's Register* in 1873. Other Castine-built ships sold abroad during the Civil War included the *Adams* and the *Samuel Adams*.

One might suspect that the culmination of the Civil War and a return to competitive shipping rates would have resulted in many of these vessels being repurchased. That was not the case, however, due to a 1797 statute which prohibited ships sold abroad from returning to the American flag. Attempts to repeal this law were unsuccessful, and the proud American merchant fleet, which had been second only to Britain's before the Civil War, would never recover.[59] Records indicate that only seven vessels were built in Castine after 1865, consisting of five schooners, one brig and one barkentine.

---

58. George W. Dalzell, *The Flight From The Flag, The Continuing Effect of the Civil War Upon the American Carrying Trade*, (Chapel Hill: The University of North Carolina Press, 1940), 239, 241, 246, 247.
59. Ibid., 249.

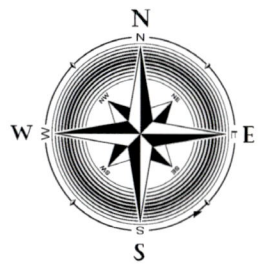

Ship *Ostervald*: Burned at Sea— Captain and Cash Held Hostage

The ship *Ostervald* was built at Castine in 1853 by Alexander N. Noyes. She was 950 tons with dimensions of 168' x 35' x 17'. Owners were William Jarvis, 4/24; John H. Jarvis, 4/24; Frederick H. Jarvis, 4/24; Lydia D. Jarvis, 3/24; Samuel Adams, 3/24; Hezekiah Williams, 3/24; and Francis H. Jarvis, 3/24; of Castine.

The *Ostervald* engaged in the typical trade of the day for five years until she caught fire and sank on a voyage from New Orleans to Liverpool in May 1858 with a cargo of 1,147 bales of cotton, 6,972 barrels of flour and 6,000 staves. The following account of the disaster was reported in the New Orleans *Times Picayune*:

Thomas Willes, Ship *Carl*, silk embroidery, undated. Courtesy Bremen State Archive, Bremen, Germany.

The bark Harriet Spaulding, Capt. Booker, arrived at the levee yesterday, having on board the two mates and sixteen men, composing the crew of the ship Ostervald, Capt. Jarvis, hence for Liverpool, which was burned at sea on the 7th inst., when about 250 miles distant from the Balize. We learn from Mr. S. Leech, first officer, that the fire was discovered at 7 o'clock A. M. by the steward of the ship, while attending to his duties in the cabin, by feeling the excessive heat penetrating the floor. All hands were called to duty, and after a consultation it was deemed advisable to place the $25,000 specie, which was on freight, together with the dunnage[60] of the men, into the small boats, and then to undertake the saving of the ship if possible. The fire in the meantime made such headway, having burned through the decks, that the captain was forced to abandon the ship. The Bremen ship Carl was in com-

---

60. Balize is a settlement near the mouth of the Mississippi River. Specie is money in coin. Dunnage is the personal belongings of the crew.

pany with the Ostervald at the time, and went to her assistance. The Captain, after taking on board Capt. Jarvis and the crew, commenced to strip the Ostervald of all the sails that could be got at readily, taking the topgallant sails, jibs, all the hawsers, the bell etc., together with the $25,000 specie, and the sailors' clothing.

Capt. Booker states that when he first discovered the Ostervald, it was about 9 o'clock A. M. He was then on the larboard tack standing southward. He thought it was a steamer, but, on going aloft, he saw that it was a ship on fire, and made for her; but before reaching her the mizzen mast had burnt and fallen over, and the whole vessel was in a light blaze by mid-day. The Bremen ship Carl bore down for him, and placed the whole of the men, with their effects on his vessel.

We regret to state that Capt. Jarvis was compelled by the Captain of the ship Carl to remain on board his ship, with the specie, and when the boats containing his crew were pushing off, he remarked to them that he saw no reason why he should be held prisoner on a foreign vessel, and forced to go to a foreign port.

The ship Ostervald was of 900 tons burthen, was six years old, and belonged to Capt. Jarvis and brother, residents of Castine, Maine. We understand she was partly insured in Boston and New York. The cargo was insured in Liverpool. [61]

The *New Orleans Daily Crescent* also reported some interesting information regarding the demise of the *Ostervald*.

There was some talk yesterday about the captain of the ship Ostervald (which vessel was destroyed by fire on the passage for Liverpool, 250 miles outside the Balize) being carried prisoner to Europe by the vessel (the Bremen ship Carl) which rescued the crew, and transferred all but the captain to the brig Harriet Spalding, arrived here. This is a very queer proceeding; however, the good Bremen ship and captain can be held accountable for damages. The inquiry is, did the good ship Ostervald have on freight $25,000 in specie for Liverpool, and does it pay to ship specie hence to Liverpool at this time from this port? Quien sabe? [62,63]

The Captain of the ship *Carl*, no doubt, forced Captain Jarvis and the $25,000 in cash to sail to Germany to ensure he received his rightful share of the salvage which by maritime law would include half of the value of recovered freight and cash on board.

Trade during the 19th century was commonly conducted in silver currency alternatively known as the "Spanish Dollar" the "Eight Royal Coin", or "Piece of Eight." Discoveries of rich silver deposits in Spanish new world territories led to these coins also being minted in Bolivia, Peru, Mexico, Colombia, Guatemala and Chile. It was likely that the $25,000 on board the *Ostervald* was denominated in this currency. The term "Pieces of Eight" came from earlier days when these coins were cut into eight pieces or "bits" each consisting of one eighth of a dollar. Spanish dollars were preferred to United States silver dollars, which had been issued since 1792, because Spanish dollars were heavier and cast from higher grade silver (27.468 grams of silver versus 27.0 grams for U.S. silver dollars). Spanish dollars remained legal tender in United States until the Coinage Act of 1857 prohibited the use of foreign currency. [64,65]

---

61. *Times Picayune*, 14 May, 1858.
62. "Who knows?"
63. *New Orleans Daily Crescent*, May 15, 1858.
64. Murray Rothbard, *Commodity Money in Colonial America*, LewRockwell.com.
65. David A. Martin, *The Changing Role of Foreign Money in the United States, 1782–1857.* Journal of Economic History, vol. 37, No. 4 (1977), 1009–1027.

Silver trade coins from this period were found in the Whitney house and are shown below.

France 1 Ecu	Mexico 8 Real	Mexico 8 Real	Mexico 8 Real	Mexico 8 Real
1784	1807	1809	1818	1842
Louis XVI	Charles IV	Ferdinand VII	Ferdinand VII	

19th century trade coins. Private Collection.

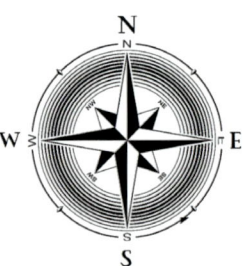

Ship *J. P. Whitney*: Castine–New Orleans Connection and Sinking in the Indian Ocean

Unknown artist, ship *J. P. Whitney*. Courtesy National Maritime Museum, Greenwich, London, England, Macpherson Collection. Here shown in the Gulf of Naples with Mount Vesuvius visible off the starboard bow. The flag atop the mainmast identifies her as the *J. P. Whitney* but the Marryat Code hoist at the mizzen head incorrectly reads 5,1,7,8 under the 3rd distinguishing pennant when it should read 6,2,1,0 under the 2nd distinguishing pennant. Ship portrait painters commonly made errors when representing Marryat Codes. Built at Castine in 1853 by J. H. Noyes, she was 874 tons with dimensions of 161' x 34' x 17'. Owners were Daniel Johnston, 1/16; Samuel Adams, 2/16; C. A. Cate & Co., 1/16; of Castine; and Leonard J. Whiting, 4/16; and J. P. Whitney & Co., 8/16; of New Orleans. Her home port was New Orleans except for the Civil War years when her home port shifted to Castine to escape the blockades.

The ship *J. P. Whitney* is a manifestation of the close relationship that developed between the ports of Castine and New Orleans. This was largely due to J. P. Whitney & Company, of New Orleans, founded by John Perkins Whitney and his brother Samuel, who were nephews of Captain Henry Whitney of Castine. J. P. Whitney & Co. was initially constituted to import cured fish from Castine but over time expanded into the cotton export business and other commercial enterprises. Although Samuel and his wife Rebecca drowned while crossing the Penobscot Bay in March of 1846, and John died in New Orleans of scarlet fever in 1848, the business continued, and J. P. Whitney & Co. was not dissolved until 1859. The Castine built ship *J. P. Whitney* was named in honor of John Perkins Whitney who was instrumental in establishing the very profitable New Orleans trade connections for Castine merchants.

After sixteen years trading between America, Europe and the Far East, the ship *J. P. Whitney* met her fate on April 10, 1869. She departed Calcutta in mid-February under the command of Captain Ober and nothing was heard from her for more than seven and a half months. All were presumed dead and Captain Ober's estate had been settled. On October 3, 1869, the following cable from Calcutta was received in Boston, "Ober safe. Inform friends." One can only imagine the joy of Ober's family and the renewed hope for the families of the crew wishing that their loved ones had also survived. A harrowing account of the events that took place between the ship's foundering and the sending of the cablegram were recorded by passenger A.N. Shalders, who survived the ordeal:

The American ship, J. P. Whitney, of 1,000 tons burthen, owned in New Orleans, United States, left Calcutta on the 15th day of February last, bound to Mauritius with a cargo of rice consigned to J. Allarakia, of Port Louis, and was lost at sea on the 10th April last in lat. 15 4 S. long. 71 40 E. Part of the crew of which vessel have arrived at this port recently. The following facts connected with the ship, and the marvelous escape of part of the crew together with their sufferings may not be uninteresting to many of your readers.

After the ship left Calcutta she experienced light variable winds, with occasional squalls and heavy seas, till the 8th of April when the barometer indicated a change, and the whole appearance of the heavens wore that of an approaching storm and everything was done that a careful and experienced ship master would do under such circumstances; towards night the wind increased to a gale with heavy seas, which continued till the following day, the 9th, when it blew a hurricane, and the waves broke over her continually. At 3 ½ P. M. a heavy sea struck the ship, and carried away the bulwarks on both sides fore and aft sweeping her decks, and at the same time stove in the fore part of the cabin and after part of the main house, and washed everything upon deck overboard. The ship now labored very heavily as there was a confused cross sea which rendered the ship almost unmanageable.

The pumps were sounded, and it was found, that the ship had sprung a leak. All hands were immediately employed in pumping the ship. At noon the gale had moderated a little but the leak was gaining very fast there being at the time 5 feet of water in the hold. Orders were now given to throw overboard some of the cargo which was immediately done from the hatch in the Carpenter's room, as there was too much water washing over her decks to open her main hatch, and at the time she was leaking fearfully…During the night of the 9th the sea moderated considerably. The pumps were kept going all night, but on the morning of the 10th the breeze had abated but there was a heavy cross sea running.

All hands were engaged in pumping the ship, and throwing cargo overboard, and every effort was made to save the ship.

After all these strenuous and desperate efforts, it became clear to one and all that there was no saving the ship and efforts turned towards saving the passengers and crew:

At 9 P. M. we found nine feet of water in the hold, and the ship was rapidly settling, and all hopes of saving her were abandoned. The night was very dark, the Captain gave orders to have all the boats ready with provisions and water to leave the ship, and at 9:30 orders were given to the respective crews to lower altogether as they were afraid that they would not get clear of the ship before she sank.

The boats were lowered but in leaving the ship, two of the boats were stove in, and Mr. Rainey (2nd officer) and about twenty of the men were drowned. Soon after the boat left the ship she went down in Lat. 15.4 S. Longitude 71.40 E. The boat that contained Captain Ober was about 19 feet long, by 5 feet beam, and in her were the first Officer, Mr. Browne, and Mr. A. N. Shalders of Calcutta, a passenger with 8 seamen, and all the provisions they could take with them were 4 lbs. tins of preserved fruit and 3 of meat, 3 small loaves of bread, and about 3 ½ gallons of water. It was impossible to take anything else as the boat was loaded to her gunwale, with a very heavy sea to ride over. There they were 400 miles from Rodrigues the nearest land, which the Captain intended to steer for in the morning. The sailors were tired of rowing, and they managed to make a sail of a small cotton sheet, by which they could lighten their labour.

Unknown artist, ship *J. P. Whitney*. Here shown leaving Liverpool with the Skerries Lighthouse off the port bow. In this image, she is shown with a painted white horizontal stripe accentuating false gun ports which was a tactic used to ward off potential raiders from a distance. Private Collection.

They remained for some hours on the following morning in hopes of discovering some of the rest of the crew on portions of the wreck. The sea was strewn with pieces of wood, empty cases, portions of a chest of oranges, the Captain's trunk etc., and they thought they discovered a boat. Then they got closer, it proved to be the remainder of the boat the 2nd mate went in. There were 4 or 5 men in it, one dying; they had fixed the Captain's bedstead across it, so that it was a little more than a raft. They spoke to the poor fellows and asked whether they had seen the other boat, but they said that on leaving the ship, they had struck against it, which broke the boat, and killed Mr. Rainey the 2nd officer, and then the ship and other boats went down. Very reluctantly the Capt. gave orders to continue their course; it was very hard to leave the poor fellows to their fate, but under the circumstances, he was compelled to do so, or endanger the lives of all.

Leaving behind fellow crew members to a certain fate must have been horribly difficult and one can only imagine the feelings of all as Captain Ober's boat pulled away from this ramshackle raft. However, even the eleven souls fortunate enough to be in this boat were anything but safe:

The sea rose high with the sun, but with the sail helping the rowers they managed to make some headway. As soon as the Captain had taken a sight to ascertain their position, they had their first meal since breakfast the preceding day. It consisted of a small piece of bread and about two tablespoonfuls of water; all were served alike from the Captain to the Lascar sailors,[66] and the same economy was continued throughout the perilous voyage, as they knew not how long they might be getting to land as they were obliged to go before the wind. On Sunday the 11th the wind shifted, in the early morning, so that it was impossible to steer for Rodrigues.

Fortunately, the Captain had saved his Charts and as the wind freshened greatly he and the 1st officer consulted, and came to the conclusion that they were in the S. E. trades, and that it would be best to try to make for Diego Garcia in the Chagos Archipelago. This day a tin of preserved veal was served out which gave a spoonful all round, but unfortunately they shipped a heavy sea which got into a jug containing half a gallon of water and spoilt it, wetting their bread and drenching everyone. A shower of rain falling in the afternoon they managed to catch some in their sheet sail, and in an oilskin coat of the captain's, which relived them from the fear of being short of that article.

On Monday the 12th, they rigged up a jib sail which helped the boat along. It appeared surprising how little the Lascars seemed to suffer from thirst, but it was soon accounted for by finding that the Carpenter had taken a jar of sugar, which these men had been making very free with. The Captain gave the orders to put it aft, and for breakfast and tea they had a measure of water, and a spoonful of sugar, reserving the other things for dinner. This sugar proved a great acquisition as it satisfied hunger too.

With their makeshift sail and limited provisions, the crowded boat was pushed slowly towards what was thought to be the closest feasible destination. The unpredictable seas were not in a mood to cooperate and the situation became more perilous:

On Tuesday the 13th the waves rose so high they threatened every moment to swamp the boat. They commenced with a long swell but soon got shorter as the wind increased, and at last broke over the boat so frightfully, all thought their last hour was come.

It was with difficulty the Capt. could steer and all they could do was to bail out the water as wave after wave broke over them. Fortunately, the boat was built sharp at both ends and the Captain who was steering being very stout his broad back prevented the boat from being filled and swamped. The mast a good stout ash oar bent like a reed, and at last the Captain gave orders for all clothes to be thrown overboard to lighten the boat as they were all heavy with water. This was promptly done, shirts, coats, trowsers, boots, clothes of all description went overboard and lightened the boat very much. Though everyone felt it was a forborn hope, they all worked like men determined to struggle to the last. Stern despair was stamped on every face, a look no one will ever forget who shared that terrible voyage.

---

66. A Lascar was a sailor from South Asia, Southeast Asia, the Arab world, and other territories east of the Cape of Good Hope.

It would be useless following the daily miseries that the poor fellows suffered, they can be better imagined than described, some days with only a little sugar and water. On the twenty-first to their great joy and thankfulness they sighted the Six Islands, a distance of nearly 600 miles, after having been twelve days hovering between life and death. [67]

Mr. Lapierre the Administrator of the Six Islands went off four miles to meet the boat. Most of the men were in so weak a condition when they landed that they could scarcely stand. This gentleman took them to his own house, clothed and fed them for two months, and refused to take any remuneration.

During this time Capt. R. Dolphin, of the English brig Ibis, of this port arrived there, and offered to give them all a free passage to Mauritius which he did, feeding them well, and taking every possible care of them till their arrival at Port Luis harbor. On their passage they stopped at the Agalagar [Agalega] Islands, and were kindly entertained by the Administrator, S. C. Feuilharde, Esquire.

Such acts of generosity and kindness, fortunately for the sake of humanity to be found the world over, are yet so remarkable as to deserve special notice, and we believe it is the intention of the American Consul to lay the facts before his government that those gentlemen may receive the praise they have so highly merited.

(Signed) A. N. Shalders, Passenger on board the J. P. Whitney. [68]

This account of the *J. P. Whitney*'s demise highlights the dangers and difficulties encountered at sea at a time when weather forecasts and telecommunications did not exist. If ships in distress were not sighted and assisted by passing vessels, life boats and an uncertain fate were the only options.

---

67. Six Islands, also known as the Egmont Islands, which are part of the Chagos Archipelago near the equator in the Indian Ocean.

68. John Richard Ober, *A Yankee Shipmaster*, vol. 47. (Boston: Stone and Webster Journal, 1930).

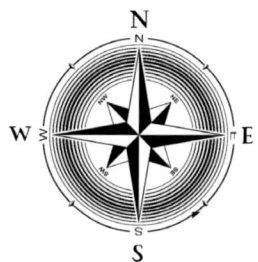

Ship *Samuel Adams*: Bamboozled in Bombay and Assistance on the High Seas

The ship *Samuel Adams* was built in Castine in 1854 by Samuel Noyes for a cost of $73,000. She was the largest ship built at Castine with a displacement of 1178 tons and dimensions of 184' x 37' x 19'. Owners were William Witherle, 1/4; Samuel Adams, 1/4; Leonard Gay, 1/8; Samuel Noyes, 1/12; Samuel T. Noyes, 1/12; J. Haskell Noyes, 1/12; of Castine; and O. H. Hilliard, 1/8; of Bangor.

She was named after Samuel Adams, a successful Castine merchant and ship owner whose general store and dock were located close to where Eaton's Boatyard is today. The ship was likely named after him in honor of his retirement from a successful business career after selling his company stock to his sons, Samuel and Alfred. When his son Samuel died in 1861, he purchased the stock back and continued in business until 1872.[69] There is a stained-glass window in the younger Samuel's memory in the Trinitarian Congregational Parish in Castine where Samuel Adams, Sr., served as deacon for most of his adult life.

Obtaining crews was always a difficult task and sailors were required to honor their contracts which often included clauses of duration and a specified number of voyages. When crew members broke their contracts, the accepted practice was for local authorities to come to the aid of the captain by arresting or otherwise punishing the offenders in order to maintain the required discipline. When a ship arrived in a foreign port and word was out that authorities were turning a blind eye to the enforcement of maritime law, crews would jump ship or make extortionate demands understanding that the captain was at a disadvantage.

The following letter describing such a situation was drafted in the port of Bombay in 1855 by interested American parties including Leonard Gay of Castine, master of the ship *Samuel Adams*.

Bombay, May 26, 1855.

To The Hon. Chamber Of Commerce Of New-york:

Gentlemen—The undersigned, captains of American ships, and Americans, now in Bombay, beg to lay before your honorable body the present existing state of affairs regarding the manner in which assistance or protection is refused by the government of India to the United States Consul at this port, and through him to

---

69. George Augustus Wheeler, *History of Castine, Penobscot and Brooksville, Maine* (Cornwall, New York: Privately Printed, 1923).

Grant's Building Bombay, 1855. Courtesy The British Library Board, London, England.

American life and property. English ships arriving at this port are, in case of mutiny, or refusal of duty on the part of their crews, protected by the police authorities, who imprison the men on shore; whereas American ships under the same circumstances are refused all protection or relief from the local authorities whatever, and are often prevented or deterred from using such means on board as the security of the lives of the officers or safety of the ship and cargo demands.

The ship Napoleon, Captain Chatfield, of Boston, arrived at this port on the 29th day of May, 1854, and soon afterwards the crew refused duty unless a month's pay was given them and liberty to go on shore for a few days. This, of course, was refused; but the crew, who had shipped in Boston, to perform the whole voyage, now insisted upon having their discharge, and the captain applied to the Consul for assistance. The Consul, in turn, applied to the local authorities, but was refused any assistance whatever; and, in the meantime, the crew had procured liquor and became riotous on board. They assaulted the captain, and maltreated him severely, compelled the second mate to save his life by jumping overboard, and took mutinous possession of the ship. The Consul then applied to the Commander-in-Chief of the Indian Navy, who, as a matter of courtesy, sent a file of Marines on board, and had four of the ring-leaders put in close irons and removed on board one of the ships of war. The Consul afterwards paid the passage of these four men to Calcutta out of his own private purse, with the expectation of the Consul at this port forwarding them to the U. S. for trial . . .

In view of the increasing number of American ships visiting this port, we venture, in behalf of the commercial interests of the United States, to call your attention to the abuses and neglect which our said interest suffers in this port . . . The object of a voyage is thus often completely frustrated, as, in case of shipment of a native crew, we are bound by government, under heavy bonds, to return the seaman to India, which, of course, cripples us pursuing any voyage we may think best for the interests of the owners.

We therefore pray that you will consult your own interest, as well as the interest of the entire community of the United States, by pressing upon our government the necessity of immediately effecting a consular convention between the Governments of the United States and Great Britain, by which more ample powers maybe conferred upon the United States consuls in the dominions of the East India Company , , , We all unite in paying a tribute of respect to Edward Ely, Esq., the United States Consul at this port . . . and we consider that if his powers were more unlimited, much of the present abuse of our interests would be remedied, and the honor of the United States government more fully sustained.

Praying that you will give this subject your earnest attention, we remain, gentlemen,
Your obedient servants,

GEO. S. BREWSTER, *ship David Brown, New-York.*
B. W. TUCKER, *ship Swallow, New-York.*
E. BURR BROWN, *New-York.*
JOHN G. PENDLETON, *bark John Gardner, Boston.*
LEONARD GAY, *ship Samuel Adams, Castine, Me.*
HOLLIS MOORE, *ice house, Bombay.*
B. T. MARRIOTT, *Baltimore.*[70]

The minutes of the New York City Chamber of Commerce record a motion to submit this letter to the Secretary of State for further consideration and action.

Evidence that ships looked out for each other during times of difficulty is borne out in an account from the ship *Caroline* which ran into serious trouble just north of the equator on a voyage from England to Australia loaded with emigrants. The ship *Samuel Adams*, commanded by Captain Gay, came to their rescue:

The Caroline
The arrival of this Government emigrant ship in our waters yesterday was announced at the very early hour of 4 a.m. by the discharge of two of the ship's guns. The boats of those who attempted to board were guided, on leaving the Semaphore beach, by a faint light in the direction of Holdfast Bay, and supposed that the vessel making the signals was the screw steamship Bosphorus, bringing from Melbourne the English mails expected per Boomerang.[71]
On reaching the Caroline they were informed that the guns had been fired in consequence of the desertion of five of the crew who had decamped in the life-boat belonging to the ship, which they had cut from the davits.

During the voyage light winds were chiefly prevalent but the 8th February, in lat. 2° 53' N., long. 24° 23' W., was marked by a very appalling occurrence. At 3 a.m. on that day a flash of chain lightning struck the ves-

---

70. C. T. Emmet, *The Monthly Nautical Magazine and Quarterly Review*, vol 2. April to September (1855).
71. *Boomerang* was an emigrant ship.

sel, carrying away the fore and main topmasts, and the foretop, foretopgallant yards, fore and mizzen royal yards, mizen-topgallantmast, and topmast-crosstrees, splitting the foretopsail, foresail, topgallantsail, and completely destroying two royals. This sad accident, for the time, completely crippled the ship.

Happily however, on the same day, at 9 a.m., the Caroline boarded the American ship Samuel Adams. The commander, Capt. Gay, not only acted in a most seamanlike manner but evinced his kindness and generosity in various ways and presented the master of the Caroline with the only spare topmast he had on board.

The emigrants on board the Caroline, who seem to have been very carefully selected, are all English. The classification is as follows:—

Adults	*245*
Children under 14	*106*
Infants	*15*
	366
Births during the voyage	*6*
	372
Deaths, 12 infants and 2 adults	*14*
Total to disembark	*358* [72]

Life at sea for sailors, who spent considerable time climbing in the rigging to set and furl sails in weather of all conditions, was a dangerous occupation. A rather sad event for the *Samuel Adams* was recorded in 1861:

Ship Samuel Adams, Mead, from Liverpool, reports 14th inst., at 6 A.M. off the light ship, John Jones, seaman, of Liverpool, Eng., aged 16 years, while chasing a bird, and when in the mizzen chains, lost his balance, fell overboard, and was lost. A boat was immediately lowered, in order to save him, but it swamped. Life preservers were thrown to him, but he failed to reach them. [73,74]

The ship *Samuel Adams* was indeed a world trader with recorded voyages to ports including Adelaide, Australia; Callao, Peru; and Bombay, India. She was sold during the Civil War in October 1864 to British interests and hailed from Newport, England until 1871.

---

72. *South Australian Register*, April 26, 1855.
73. Captain Mead.
74. *New York Times*, May 17, 1861.

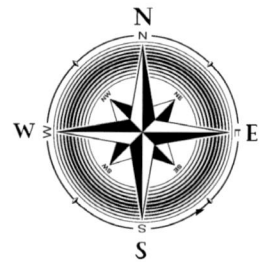

Ship *Hezekiah Williams*: Short Life in Timber and Salt

Ship *Hezekiah Williams* on the stocks at the Noyes and Perkins shipyard in Castine from *Sailing Days on the Penobscot*, Wasson and Colcord, p. 318 (Salem, Marine Research Society, 1932). She was built at Castine in 1856 by Alexander N. Noyes and was 877 tons with dimensions of 163' x 34' x 17'. Owners were William Witherle, 5/16; Joseph Wescott, 5/16; Hezekiah Williams, 2/16; David L. Stevens, 2/16; Isaiah Wescott, 1/16; of Castine and William Vose, 1/16; of St. Louis.

A new trade route for American shipping was initiated in 1849 when Canadian ports were opened to foreign vessels. This involved carrying timber from Canada to Britain and returning with salt required for the Penobscot fishing industry.

The *Hezekiah Williams* was built for Witherle & Co. to partake in this trade. She was named after prominent Castine resident and Congressman, Hezekiah Williams, who had died in 1856. Today a stained-glass window given in his remembrance can be found in the Trinitarian Congregational Parish on Main Street in Castine. Although built in Castine, the *Hezekiah Williams* was designed by a well-known Boston clipper ship designer, Samuel Hartt Pook, with ideal proportions for the salt and timber trade. [75] After being launched she was sent to St. John, New Brunswick, Canada, to be loaded with timber.

The crew of the *Hezekiah Williams* on this maiden voyage included some wholesome young men from Maine. When landing at the port of St. John, their visit to the Marine Hall on October 6, 1856, was recorded by the minister of the St. John Chaplaincy:

Meetings at the Marine Hall, occur every Sabbath …. The 2 o'clock prayer meeting is always taken up by sea faring persons who hope in the mercy of God.

Our Bethel meeting on the third Sabbath of Sept. was unusually good. Several ministers were present and took an active part in the exercises.

The first delivered a very searching discourse, followed by addresses from the other two brethren. The Hall was crowded, and among them were more than sixty sailors; and it is evident that they did not all hear in vain, in as much as nine returned, to understand the way to heaven more perfectly. These belonged to the ship Hez. Williams, and were all sons of Maine.

We gave them the best instruction we could, and furnished them with such tracts as they wanted, with which they left in company for their ship; where may it please God to give them convicting and soul saving grace. We could not suppress fervent breathing at the mercy seat, that those seamen may know God, whom to know is life eternal.[76]

From St. John, the *Hezekiah Williams* sailed to Liverpool with her load of timber and took on cargo for the port of Philadelphia. Unfortunately, on her return voyage she met her fate in February 1857 at Port Joli, Nova Scotia. She has the dubious distinction of being the shortest lived Castine-built ship with less than one year at sea. Her crew members must have been thankful for their church visit while at St. John, because they all survived the wreck.

The following account of the demise of the *Hezekiah Williams* is from the *New York Times* in 1857:

The Ship Hezekiah Williams, with a valuable cargo, from Liverpool, England, for Philadelphia, went ashore on Saturday night at Port Joli, she was bilged, and her masts are gone. The crew were saved.[77]

---

75. Wayne M. O'Leary, "The Maine Transatlantic Salt Trade in the Nineteenth Century," *The American Neptune*, vol. 47, No. 2, (1987), 100.

76. *The Sailor's Magazine*, vol. 29–30, 1856.

77. "Marine Disasters," *New York Times*, March 11, 1857.

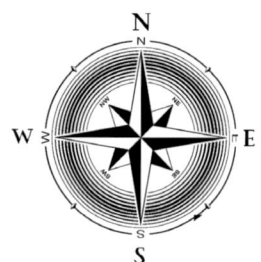

Ship *Edward Hyman*: Unfortunate Timing and The Cook's Revenge

Ship *Edward Hyman*, glass plate copy-negative, c. 1890, photographer William Sargent. Courtesy Castine Historical Society. Here shown inward bound to Liverpool off Anglesey with the Skerries Lighthouse off the starboard bow. She was built at Castine in 1856 by Samuel T. Noyes and was 1056 tons with dimensions of 181' x 36' x 18'. Owners were Richard B. Sumner, 3/8; and Mary H. Hyman, 2/8; of New Orleans. Charles A. Cate, 1/24; John W. Dresser, 1/24; Daniel Johnston, 1/8; Francis A. Whiting, 1/16; of Castine and Samuel K. Whiting, 1/16; of Boston. Her home port was New Orleans.

The construction of the ship *Edward Hyman* at Castine was initiated in 1855 by Captain Leonard Whiting for himself and other Castine and New Orleans investors. Previously, Leonard had been based out of New Orleans as master and part owner of the ships *European* and *J. P. Whitney*. He had retired from the sea and was adding ownership in the *Edward Hyman* to his portfolio. The ship was named after Edward Hyman, one of the principals of J. P. Whitney and Co., who had died earlier in 1855.

Unfortunately, Captain Whiting's health was deteriorating from an old injury incurred at sea when he was thrown against bilge pumps during a gale. He died in Castine in November 1855 at the age of 45. Frances Whitney Whiting, his 33-year-old widow, was left with two young children and bills to pay, for what was now her share of the unfinished *Edward Hyman*. Samuel Kidder Whiting, Leonard's younger brother, was executor of his will and immediately lent his assistance by purchasing half of her share in the ship:

I think it best to have all your bills paid in Castine at once. I should feel better myself in having every one paid at once. I can furnish the money now. Leonard and I always agreed about being in debt to others and I can not bear the idea now of having his estate owe any one who wants their pay—for I know very well if I had been taken away first my dear brother would at once have done the same for me. So my dear sister, do not hesitate a moment to draw on me for all your wants at once for I shall take great pleasure in paying it.

I will take the new ship with you. I believe it will be as good property as I can invest in at present and I have the funds in Bank to meet my part of the payments.[78]

After receiving assistance for the pressing need to cover bills, Frances' partial ownership of the ships *European*, *J. P. Whitney* and *Edward Hyman* contributed sufficient profits to comfortably support her and the children while they lived in the Whitney house on the Castine Town Common. In 1858, Frances married her brother-in-law, Samuel Kidder Whiting, after his wife succumbed to a long illness. They continued living in the stately Whitney house and investing in sailing vessels for the remainder of their lives.

Records from an 1865 court case involving crew members on the ship *Edward Hyman* highlight the dangers of making enemies while at sea. The defendant in this case, Michael G. Seminary, "the colored cook on board the ship *Edward Hyman*" was charged with attempting to poison Seaman William Brown on a voyage from Shields, England, to New York.

It all started when Brown was sitting on the main hatchway spinning a yarn for the entertainment of his fellow crew. The cook came out of the bunk area and approaching them said, "God damn your eyes." When Brown asked who he was talking to he said, "you." In response Brown told him to step out on the deck and if he wanted anything from him, he could have it there and then. The cook responded that Brown "didn't fight fair" and said that when he found Brown sleeping, he would "kill him right off"—then he returned to his bunk. The next morning, they again exchanged words with the cook telling Brown that he would "kick him in the breast."

Brown testified that on the morning of the 27th of October he was at the wheel at about five o'clock, his usual time for getting coffee. Another man took his place and he went to the galley and asked the cook for some coffee. There was no answer from the cook. Brown went to the forecastle and then came back to the galley where the cook gave him a cup containing coffee and asked him if he wanted some sugar. Brown answered that he did not and went back to the forecastle, drank the coffee and resumed his position at the wheel. He soon became sick and had to "heave up." He was relieved at the wheel and went to the forecastle and had to "heave up all the forenoon." No one else drank the coffee and when asked, the cook denied that he had put anything in it. The cook, who had also become ill, was put in irons.

---

78. Letter from Samuel Kidder Whiting to Frances Whitney Whiting, January 1856. Castine Historical Society.

Captain H. W. Rhodes testified that Brown "was taken with vomiting, turned pale, and had extended eyes" after drinking the coffee. The cup was brought to him by the Mate and he witnessed a white substance in the bottom of it. The captain stated the cook had also become sick, but with different symptoms, and had denied that he poisoned Brown. Based on the evidence, the cook was kept in irons for two days and became so sick that he was put in the hatch house and kept there until they arrived in port.[79],[80],[81]

The cup, which had been locked in a chest since the incident, was taken to a chemist for analysis upon arrival at port. The presence of poison was confirmed. Michael G. Seminary was found guilty of attempting to poison William Brown and was handed down a sentence of three years in prison.

The ship *Edward Hyman* engaged in European and South American trade from her home port of New Orleans, including sailing for the Regular Line in 1858 for agents J. P. Whitney and Co. She survived the war as an American-flagged vessel and in 1874 was sold to French owners. The *Edward Hyman* sailed from a home port of Nantes, France through 1879 recording a respectable life at sea of twenty-three years.

79. "The Poisoning Case on Shipboard; United States Commissioner's Office," *New York Times*, November 26, 1865.

80. *Sacramento Daily Union*, December 25, 1865.

81. "Law reports.; Court of Appeals Calendar, January Term, 1866," *New York Times*, December 31, 1865.

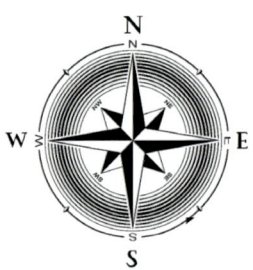

Ship *Castine*: Persecution of the Steward

Attributed to Francis Hustwick, ship *Castine*, after 1857. Oil on board. Courtesy Butler Institute of American Art, Youngstown, Ohio, museum purchase, 1929. The ship *Castine* here shown inward bound to Liverpool at the western entrance to the River Mersey with Perch Rock Fort and Lighthouse visible off the starboard bow. She was built at Castine in 1857 by Samuel T. Noyes and was 962 tons with dimensions of 170' x 35' x 18'. Owners were R. B. Sumner, 5/8, of New Orleans and Samuel Adams, 1/8; Samuel Noyes, 1/24; J. Haskell Noyes, 1/24; Samuel T. Noyes, 1/24 of Castine, and James Simpson, 1/8, of Chelsea, Massachusetts.

The following announcement of ship *Castine*'s launch was published in New Orleans in April, 1857:
> *Launch of a New Orleans Ship. On the 25th ult., the ship Castine was launched from the yard of Messrs. S. & J. H. Noyes & Co., of Castine Maine. This ship, of about 1000 tons burthen, was built of good materials, and*

of superior workmanship, for Messrs. J. P. Whitney & Co., of New Orleans, and others, and is to be commanded by Capt. Jas. Simpson, of Chelsea, Mass, late of ship Meridian. She is intended for the general freighting business.[82]

In March of 1853 newly elected President Franklin Pierce appointed Nathaniel Hawthorne, his friend for many years and author of his pre-election biography, US Consul of Liverpool. Hawthorne was already an author of note having published *The Scarlet Letter* in 1850. Due to the significant volume of trade between the US and the port of Liverpool, the consul role there was considered the most lucrative Foreign Service position at the time.

While in Liverpool, Hawthorne concerned himself with consular duties which frequently involved hearing the complaints of sailors from American ships. Soon after his arrival the following dispatch describes those waiting to meet with him at the Consulate:

The staircase and passageway were often thronged, of a morning, with a set of beggarly and piratical-looking scoundrels (I do no wrong to our own countrymen in styling them so, for not one in twenty was a genuine American), purporting to belong to our mercantile marine, and chiefly composed of Liverpool Blackballers and the scum of every maritime nation of earth; such being the seamen by whose assistance we then disputed the navigation of the world with England. These specimens of a most unfortunate class of people were shipwrecked crews in quest of a bed, board, and clothing; individuals asking permits for the hospital; bruised and bloody wretches complaining of ill-treatment by their officers; drunkards, desperadoes, vagabonds, and cheats, perplexingly intermingled with an uncertain proportion of reasonably honest men. All of them (save here and there a poor devil of a kidnapped landsman in his shore-going rags) wore red flannel shirts, in which they had sweltered or shivered throughout the voyage, and all required consular assistance in one form or another.[83]

Charles Osgood, *Portrait of Nathaniel Hawthorne*, 1840. Courtesy Peabody Essex Museum, Salem, Massachusetts, 1993.121459. Photo by Mark Sexton and Jeffrey Dykes.

Another of Consul Hawthorne's dispatches from Liverpool deals with a complaint by George Maudluff [Mandluff], an African American steward on the ship *Castine*, against Captain James Simpson from Chelsea, Massachusetts:

Liverpool, 18 September 1857

Sir,

I forward herewith certain depositions taken before me in the case of George Maudluff steward of the ship "Castine." You will perceive by them that while the ship was lying in the port of Castine in April last the Master Captain James Simpson committed a violent and bloody assault upon the person of the steward without any ade-

---

82. *Times Picayune*, April 9, 1857.

83. Nathaniel Hawthorne, *Our Old Home, and English Note-books*, v. 1, (Cambridge: Houghton, Mifflin and Company, The Riverside Press, 1891), 19–20.

quate cause. Captain Simpson himself in a personal interview which I had with him substantially admitted having perpetrated the assault and was unable to justify it on any more definite grounds than an alleged insolence in the look or tone of the steward. The injuries sustained by the latter were serious, as was evidenced by the scars still remaining on his head and arm.

There appears to have been no other ill treatments of the steward on the part of the Captain until after the ship arrived in Liverpool when in consequence of his making complaint of the above facts to me Captain Simpson again violently assaulted him and the steward deserted from the vessel.

As the first and more desperate assault was committed in one of our ports and as the steward then (whether through ignorance or for whatever other reason) failed to bring the case before a Magistrate I might perhaps have felt myself justified in passing the matter over provided there had been no evidence of an enduring malevolence on Captain Simpson's part. But the second assault appeared to me to imply that the Captain cherished resentment against the steward which might on slight occasion break forth in further violence and this impression was strengthened by the tone of the Captain's remarks made personally to myself in reference to the reason and the facts.

Under such circumstances I considered that my duty required me to view the second assault in the light thrown on it by the first; and I therefore ordered the discharge of the steward with payment of three months' advance wages, conceiving it better for both parties that they should be separated. Captain Simpson declining to comply with the order as regarded the payment of advance wages I refused to deliver the ship's register. I feel it proper to say that Captain Simpson's general treatment of his crew appears to have been unexceptionable and that he seemed to me on the whole a kind hearted man, but to be afflicted with a temper easily kindled to violence and not easily pacified. The man being colored I could not send him to New Orleans where the vessel has gone and have sent him to Boston.[84]

Captain Simpson died in 1858 on the *Castine*'s return voyage from Liverpool to New Orleans as the ship was approaching the mouth of the Mississippi River.[85] The ship *Castine* went on to have a fruitful career for her Castine and New Orleans owners trading for 26 years at ports across the Atlantic and Pacific oceans. She was sold in 1884 to owners in Bremen, Germany, which was her home port until 1889.

---

84. John R. Byers, Jr., ed., *Consular Dispatches of Nathaniel Hawthorne,* (Salem: Essex Institute Historical Collections, 1977), 319–321 .

85. Joseph W. Porter, ed., *The Maine Historical Magazine,* vol. 6, (1891), 205.

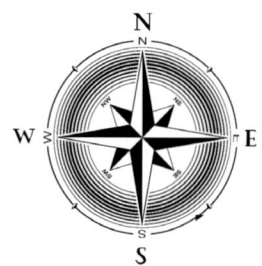

Ship *Picayune*: Cotton Screwers and Tragedy Far from Home

Attributed to Francis Hustwick, ship *Picayune*. Courtesy Louisiana State Museum, New Orleans, Louisiana. Here shown inward bound to Liverpool at the western entrance to the River Mersey with Perch Rock Fort and Lighthouse visible off the starboard bow. Built in 1857 by Samuel T. Noyes, she was the last ship built at Castine. She was 1081 tons with dimensions of 172' x 35' x 18'. Owners were Samuel T. Noyes, 1/12; J. Haskell Noyes, 1/12, of Castine and R. B. Sumner, 3/4, of New Orleans. Her home port was New Orleans.

Cargoes that created most of the wealth for Castine merchants and ship owners were fish and cotton. Salted fish from the Penobscot District brought good prices in the south as did cotton delivered to

European ports. Fish was transported in barrels or boxes which were tightly packed into the ship's holds. Cotton was transported in bales which had more flexibility than wooden containers and therefore could be compressed into the hold to maximize the cargo and resulting profits. The following is a description of loading cotton at New Orleans in 1850:

New Orleans at this time, was the great shipping port of the South for exporting cotton to Europe, although Mobile, Savannah and Charleston also shipped great quantities. In the winter months, all along the levees at New Orleans lay tiers of shipping of all nationalities, loading cotton for the northern ports of the United States, as well as the various ports of Europe. The river front is shaped like a crescent, and from this fact New Orleans takes its name of the "Crescent City." For miles along the banks, or levees, extends the shipping, lying in tiers, loading cotton, staves, or tobacco, but principally cotton. The bales were rolled from the levee by the stevedores' gangs, generally roustabout darkies, up the staging, and tumbled on deck and down the hold, where they were received by gangs of cotton-screwers, there being as many gangs in the ship's hold as could work to advantage. The bales were placed in tiers, and when they would apparently hold no more, with the aid of planks and pow-

Cotton screwer gang compressing cotton bales into a ship's hold. Unknown Source.

erful cotton-screws, several bales would be driven in where it would appear to a novice impossible to put one.

Four men to a screw constituted a gang, and it was a point of honor to screw as many bales in a ship's hold as could possibly be crammed in, and in some cases even springing the decks upwards, such a power was given by the screw. All this work was accompanied by a song, often improvised and sung by the "chantie" man, the chorus being taken up by the rest of the gang. Each gang possessed a good "chantie" singer, with a fine voice. The chorus would come in with vim, and every pound in the muscles of the gang would be thrown into the handle-bars of

the cotton-screwers, and a bale of cotton would be driven in where there appeared to be but a few inches of space.

The songs or "chanties" from hundreds of these gangs of cotton-screwers could be heard all along the river front, day after day, making the levees of New Orleans a lively spot. As the business of cotton-screwing was dull during the summer months, the majority of the gangs, all being good sailors, shipped on some vessel that was bound to some port in Europe to pass the heated term and escape the "yellow Jack,"[86] which was prevalent at that season. When they returned in the fall they could command high wages at cotton-screwing on shipboard. Some would go to northern ports, but generally the autumn found them all back, ready for their winter's work.[87]

Although cotton was the preferred cargo that ship owners wanted to export, it was not always readily available in southern ports. We learn more about this from the letters of Castine seaman Solon J. Hanson, who sailed on the ship *Picayune* from Castine to New Orleans in November 1857 under the

---

86. Yellow fever.

87. John D. Whidden, *Ocean Life in The Old Sailing Days, From Forecastle to Quarter-deck*, (Boston: Little, Brown, and Company, 1914), 96–98.

command of Captain Brooks. Arriving in New Orleans after twelve days at sea, there was no cotton available and many ships were stacked in the port waiting for cargoes. While they were waiting, the crew were assigned maintenance tasks to make the *Picayune* shine like new:

I expect we shall all have to leave the ship the times are so hard the Castine has been hauled up here most of five weeks. Capt Brooks says he shall keep us by the ship fifteen or twenty days and then if we don't get a freight he will have to discharge us but he will hate to discharge us bad enough.[88]

We have got most all discharged I think we can finish up by next Saturday. The ship looks like a fiddle everything has painted scraped and slushed from keel to truck and now they have got a lot of holystone and prayer books and we have to get down on our knees and rub rub rub all the day long. My knees have got so hard that I have a strong notion of joining the Methodist church.[89,90]

After an arduous three-month wait, the *Picayune*, shining from stem to stern and loaded with 3,667 bales of cotton, was ready to head out on a transatlantic journey to St. Petersburg, Russia:

We are all ready for sea and shall go down river tomorrow Carries 3,667 bales. I have been sick with summer complaint for a week but am some better now. Write to me the first of May. Direct to me ship. Cronstradt[91] *care of American Consul. Shall be back to York in Dec. next guess I shall come down and have a look at you then. Give my love to all.*[92,93]

After a journey of sixty-five days, the *Picayune* arrived at Kronstadt on May 24, 1858. Unfortunately, seaman Solon Hanson would never return home to his family and friends in Maine. We learn of his fate in a letter from Captain Brooks of the *Picayune* to Solon's father:

Capt John Hanson

Dear Sir

I set down to day to perform a painful duty. The "Picayune" has been in port six weeks and is now nearly loaded for Bristol Eng. Everything went on well until last week when your son Solon was taken sick. Thursday, the 8th he was about his work as usual. In the afternoon he told Mr. Wescott he had the diarrhea and he gave him some cholrea drops to stop it. The next morning he was no better but was able to set about decks under the awning until evening when he became worse. And the mate went after the doctor, who came on board and recommended sending him to the Hospital, which was done about 8 o clock in the evening. Friday, two of the boys set up with him that night. He was taken about ten with violent cramps, and all the symptoms of the cholrea. Although everything was done for him that was possible the cramps continued until the next afternoon. Saturday the 10th, about ten o clock the cramps left him and he was free from pain, and became aware that he did not have long to live.

He passed away calmly and quietly at half past one o clock , Saturday. We were all much grieved as much as if he had been a brother. He was a favorite with all on board the ship, and there is not one in the ship whose

---

88. L. J. Webster and M. A. Noah, *Letters Home from Sea. The Life and Letters of Solon J. Hanson, Down East Sailor*, (Brookline, NH: Hobblebrush Books, 2006), 90.

89. Mariners terms: keel to truck is top to bottom; holystone is soft and brittle sandstone used for scrubbing wooden decks; prayer books are smaller hollystones.

90. Letter from Solon J. Hanson to his sister, December 1857. Webster and Noah, 91.

91. Kronstadt—Island off St. Petersburg in the Gulf of Finland, just west of St Petersburg, Russia.

92. Summer complaint was a term for noncontagious diarrhea occurring in summer or autumn and prevalent during the hot weather in the southern states.

93. Letter from Solon J. Hanson to his father, March 19, 1858. Webster and Noah, 115.

death would have been so keenly felt.

We all attended his funeral yesterday at the English Church and followed the remains to the English burying ground.

I know he must be happy wherever he is. He was so stout and healthy I never once dreamed of his being taken away. The ways of the Lord are truly mysteriory [sic]. I have been to day and ordered a grave stone, with name birth place age & I have had his clothes packed up just as he left them the day before he died and will send them to Boston.[94]

Solon, like many other adventurous souls from Castine, accepted the risks of a seafaring life. He was ambitious and had a plan to rise through the ranks eventually being awarded the command of his own ship. This was not to be. Instead, he died and was buried on a distant shore, just shy of his twentieth birthday, not comforted by the family he loved but by his sea mates who shared his hopes and dreams.

The *Picayune*, during her relatively short life of nine years, primarily traded between New Orleans, Canadian and European ports. The record of her demise is reported in the *New York Times* of July 10, 1866:

The Ship Picayune, of New Orleans, Capt. Brooks, from Genoa, in ballast, for St. John, N. B., was wrecked on Duck Island, near Mt. Desert, Me., in a fog on the 5th inst. Crew saved. Ship a total loss.

---

94. Letter from Captain Brooks to Captain John Hanson, July 13, 1858. Ibid., 129–130.

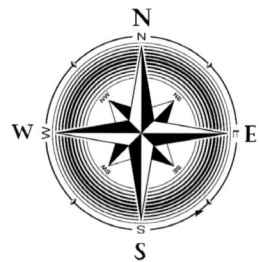

Castine and the Sea

The Castine peninsula and the ebb and flow of the waters surrounding it have been complementary since before settlers seeking a new life arrived on its rocky shores by boat. Blessed with a well-protected deep-water harbor, Castine grew from a small farming and fishing community to the flourishing center of the Penobscot Region fishing fleet during the mid-19th century. Local merchants reinvested earnings from supplying the fishing fleet into locally built wooden trading ships that engaged in profitable international trade. However, changes to trading patterns caused by the Civil War and the emergence of steam power significantly damaged the American merchant sail model. Very few Maine towns survived the downturn and renewed their marine industries. Castine's shipbuilders and fishing fleet did not vanish immediately, but the town's international commerce dwindled quickly and the local economy never fully recovered to its pre-war glory.

Stories related to Castine ships built in the 19th century provide us with insightful windows through which we can connect to the period of history that was instrumental in shaping the town. This book opens a window on the contributions of Whitneys, Whitings and Witherles as merchants, captains, and owners. Simultaneous and overlapping stories of Castine shipping would emerge from a study of Perkins, Dyer and Wescott families among others. We are also reminded that Castine's success story encompasses many lesser-known men and women whose hard work and sacrifices contributed to Castine's prosperity.

Although these glory days are

William and Sarah Witherle's house, photographed c. 1860, upper Main Street, Castine. The house was purchased by Witherle in 1828 from Captain Ebenezer Perkins who had the house built in 1807. Courtesy Castine Historical Society.

gone, the Castine of today steadfastly maintains its maritime focus. The Maine Maritime Academy trans-
forms young students into professionals for today's merchant marine at sea around the globe and shore-
side managing international trade. And Castine's streets are lined with stately homes still proudly bearing
the names of the merchants and ship captains who prospered, despite the risks, as owners and command-
ers of majestic square-rigged sailing ships.

Castine waterfront, 2014. Photograph by Richard Ames.

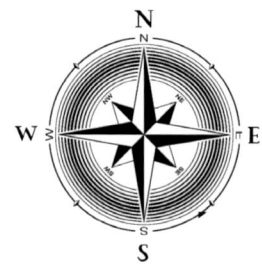

Index